Stoic Serenity

A Practical Course on Finding Inner Peace

By the same author

Epictetus' Handbook and the Tablet of Cebes: Guides to Stoic Living

Lao Tzu: Tao Te Ching

Learning the Tao: Chuang Tzu as Teacher

Time: A Philosophical Treatment

Stoic Serenity

A Practical Course on Finding Inner Peace

Keith Seddon

Lulu

First published 2006
by Lulu
www.lulu.com

© 2006 Keith Seddon

All rights reserved. No part of this book may be reprinted or reproduced or utilised in any form or by any electronic, mechanical, or other means, now known or hereafter invented, including photocopying and recording, or in any information storage or retrieval system, without permission in writing from the publishers.

ISBN 978-1-84753-817-8

Great is the struggle and divine the task.
The prize is a kingdom, freedom, serenity
and peace.

Epictetus, *Discourses* 2.18.28

CONTENTS

Preface   9

Introduction   11

    1. Good, bad and indifferent   21
    2. What is in our power   35
    3. 'Live simply' and 'Live according to nature'   50
    4. Universal nature, God and fate   67
    5. Living in society   84
    6. Impermanence, loss and death   104

Appendix 1: The Stoics on Determinism   126

Appendix 2: Striving to be Free of the Passions   135

Supplement 1: Sample Responses to Assignments   145

Supplement 2: Key to the Stoic Philosophy of Epictetus   189

Supplement 3: Conflict between Stoics and Epicurus   192

Bibliography   194

PREFACE

The course papers in this book (all the material in the numbered chapters occurring before the Appendices and the Supplements) were first published under the title *Introduction to Stoic Philosophy: The Quest for Inner Peace* by the Stoic Foundation in 2000, as unbound A4 pages, and sent out one at a time to individual students who had enrolled on the course. Students sent in their work on the exercises (one paper at a time), which was returned with responses and reactions, until the course was completed. Feedback shows that all the students who persevered to the end of the course found some benefit in it, and for a handful of people, the course appears to have affected them profoundly.

It is hoped and intended that in issuing the course as a paperback book (in almost the exact form it had when printed on loose leaves), what value it has may be appreciated by a larger audience. I very much urge readers to complete the short 'in your journal' assignments that crop up from time to time, and to engage with the book as if you really were going to send in your written responses to the exercises to a tutor, by actually recording your thoughts on paper, or on a computer, as you prefer.

The course is designed to have practical application to daily living, just as a course in Stoic philosophy would have had in ancient times; it is not technical, and is suitable for people with no prior knowledge of philosophy. From the very start, the emphasis is on encouraging readers to begin living a life that is *eudaimôn*, which is the term the ancient Greek philosophers used for 'lived well', or 'flourishing' or 'happy'. It was in this sense that the ancient philosophers sought the 'good life', and this course on finding inner peace, although not guaranteeing to anyone a life of perfect bliss, will give you the tools to think more carefully about what really matters and why, and will give you techniques for beginning to live the *eudaimôn* life.

I am very much indebted to all the students who studied under my guidance on the correspondence course, and also to the participants of the International Stoic Forum at Yahoo! Groups [http://groups.yahoo.com/group/ stoics], all of who have been instrumental in helping me engage with the Stoics and with Stoicism as a living philosophy that one may apply to the practical business of living. I am grateful to Steven Paul Hamilton for his usual thoroughness in checking the proofs.

Appendix 1, an essay on determinism, was first published in the *Volga Journal of Philosophy and Social Sciences*, in October 1999, and Appendix 2, an essay on the passions, was first published in *Practical Philosophy* in November 2000. Both essays are currently hosted by Jan Garrett at his Stoic Place website [http://www.wku.edu/~jan.garrett/stoa].

Keith Seddon

Hertfordshire, England
December 2006

INTRODUCTION

If, at the beginning of the twenty-first century, you visit a bookstore with a large philosophy section hoping to find books of practical guidance that will help you bear life's burdens and vicissitudes, you will in all likelihood be disappointed. Not wholly disappointed, to be sure. For some books on the edges of philosophy that touch or encroach upon other disciplines, such as theology or psychology, may give useful advice and offer practical solutions with regard to a wide range of topics. But what you will not find are books in the mainstream of philosophy, used in university philosophy departments around the world, with titles like *The Meaning of Life*, *How to Live Well*, or *Philosophy: The Guide to Life*.

Philosophy as a guide to life simply isn't taught any more. Although the influence of Christianity in our culture is in decline, its dominance has nevertheless been such that for centuries there was no need to ask questions like 'How should I live?' or 'How do I find peace of mind amid the turmoil of daily life?' If you live as a good Christian and follow the gospel, all will be well. At times of crisis, when things seem uncertain, puzzling, or too much to bear, all you needed to do was read the Bible and pray. Thus there was no role for philosophy in addressing these topics.

But two thousand years ago, and more, for the ancient Greeks and the ancient Romans, this was not the case. Booksellers in the ancient markets would have sold philosophy books of a wholly different character to the books in a modern bookstore. The superficial differences are obvious: the ancient books were all handwritten on papyrus scrolls (the techniques required for papermaking and for printing would not be developed for over a thousand years) – and just look at the titles! Our ancient bookseller has on his stall editions of *How to Live Amongst Men* (Diogenes), *Of Marriage, Of Freedom* (Cleanthes), *Proofs that Pleasure is Not the Good* (Chrysippus), *The Way to Wisdom, Of Wealth* (Metrodorus), *Of Love, Of Human Life, Of Just Dealing* (Epicurus), *On Anger, On Leisure, Moral Letters* (Seneca). Then, as now, philosophers addressed questions concerning the theory of knowledge, metaphysics, aesthetics, logic, and so forth, but as we can see from the titles just mentioned, philosophers were also interested in questions directly concerned with how the individual should live.

PHILOSOPHY AS A WAY OF LIFE

Speaking of the ancient schools of philosophy, the author Pierre Hadot observes:

> All schools agree that man, before his philosophical conversion, is in a state of unhappy disquiet. Consumed by worries, torn by passions, he does not live a genuine life, nor is he truly himself. All schools also agree that man can be delivered from this state.
>
> (Hadot 1995, 102)

Seeing philosophy in the way the ancients did, making it more than a matter of reading books to understand and appreciate the views of their authors (and to examine and challenge those views, just as philosophers have always done), makes it also an exercise in reorienting oneself towards life generally, and finding new and improved perspectives on one's specific concerns, to arrive eventually at a point where our worries are defeated, or our fears abolished, and our passions tempered. The endeavour to do this, and to live abiding by the insights attained, for the ancients constituted living *as a philosopher*. The term 'philosopher' designated not so much the teacher or author, but the person aiming to live the philosophical life. One of philosophy's most important figures, Socrates, said this during his trial in Athens:[1]

> I did not care for the things that most people care about – making money, having a comfortable home, high military or civil rank, and all the other activities, political appointments, secret societies, party organizations, which go on in our city... I set myself to do you – each one of you, individually and in private – what I hold to be the greatest possible service. I tried to persuade each of you to *concern himself less with what he has than with what he is*, so as to render himself as excellent and rational as possible.
> (Plato, *Apology* 36b–c, quoted in Hadot 1995, 90)

What Socrates did for himself was to find out how to make himself 'excellent and rational' – which in part at least resulted in his not caring about the sorts of things that people usually regard as of supreme importance (wealth and status, especially) – and then he set about encouraging others to do the same. Socrates is famed for his assertion that 'the unexamined life is not worth living' (*Apology* 38a). In the most general of senses, what Socrates wanted to examine is the system of values we adopt to justify what we find of importance.

And this is what we shall be doing on this course.

THE PROMISE OF STOIC PHILOSOPHY

> Shall I tell you what philosophy holds out to humanity? Counsel. One person is facing death, another is vexed by poverty, while another is tormented by wealth – whether his own or someone else's; one man is appalled by his

misfortunes while another longs to get away from his own prosperity; one man is suffering at the hands of men, another at the hands of the gods.... All mankind are stretching out their hands to you on every side. Lives that have been ruined, lives that are on the way to ruin are appealing for some help; it is to you that they look for hope and assistance.

(Seneca, *Moral Letters* 48.7–8, trans. Campbell 1969, 98)

The counsel that Seneca speaks of here, which aims to relieve people of their anxieties, and which in doing so will give to the philosopher's student a sense of profound tranquillity, is frequently conceived of (by the Stoics as well as the other philosophical schools of the Graeco-Roman period) in terms of medical imagery. That is, the philosophically unenlightened person who experiences the sorts of anxieties that Seneca enumerates is thought of as suffering a sort of sickness for which the philosopher has treatments and remedies just as the physician has prescriptions and regimes for people suffering physical illnesses.

The medical analogy is at its weakest when we note that for philosophy to effect its healing powers, it is the student themselves who must incorporate their new philosophical insights into the moment by moment business of actually leading the sort of life that first, people actually do live, and secondly, *as a life of a special sort that philosophers can attempt to live as an ideal.* So, the philosopher-teacher can guide and can give advice, but it is the job of the student to actively put that teaching into practice. The job of the teacher is to show the student how this can be done. In ancient times the teacher readily accomplished this simply by living the philosophic life, which was viewed directly by the student on a daily basis simply as a result of the student's attending their daily lessons and through personal contact at other times. Indeed, some schools accepted residential students who would actually have lived with their philosopher-teacher throughout the duration of their studies. Thus the students would have been able to see how their teacher managed their everyday affairs, how they coped with crises and lesser troubles, and how they faced the sorts of evils that in some shape or form eventually touch the lives of everyone. In short, the teacher was a model for their students.

Helping students in this way is of course impossible in a correspondence course. This is why Seneca's *Moral Letters* has been chosen as one of the set texts. The letters that Seneca wrote to Lucilius are of such a character as to show to the reader how Seneca is himself striving to adopt the philosophic life; they are written by a teacher, certainly, but all the same, the reader has a very strong sense that they are written by a fellow traveller who deeply cares that his friend should be able to make moral progress. But Seneca is a stride or two in front of his companion, and from this position he can call back, as it were, and continuously point out the benefits of the philosophic life in the hope of encouraging Lucilius – and *us*, his readers in this current age – to maintain our efforts.

From his own advanced position, Seneca announces:

> I see in myself, Lucilius, not just an improvement but a transformation.
> (Seneca, *Moral Letters* 6.1, trans. Campbell 1969, 39)

And it is a *transformation* that the philosopher-teacher aims to bring about in all their students. Once this transformation is underway, the student begins to see things quite literally differently. The sorts of troubles that Seneca mentions in the quotation at the head of this section will, once the transformation is underway, affect the student less and less. What was of concern before will have little or no influence any more. And once the transformation is complete (which the Stoics admit is an ideal state that may in fact never be experienced by anyone – though we aim for it nevertheless) these anxieties will simply and literally *not be experienced*.

From this new position everything seems different, indeed, it *is* different, and it is right to say that finding a path to this new position constitutes a transformation. The Stoics maintained that one can only be truly human once this transformation has been accomplished, and that we each of us has a responsibility to ourselves and to others to do what we can to live as close as we can to the Stoic ideal.

SET BOOKS

On this course, you will be asked to read selections from two ancient Stoic writers. These are:

> **Seneca: Letters from a Stoic** [= '*Moral Letters*'], translated by Robin Campbell, Penguin Books.
> **Marcus Aurelius: Meditations**, translated by Robin Hard, Wordsworth Editions.

It is essential that you acquire your own copies of these two books. They should be readily available from most booksellers, or from Internet bookstores, including my own Amazon bookstores at <http://astore.amazon.co.uk/stoicfoundati-21>, for the UK, and <http://astore.amazon.com/stoicfoundati-20> for the USA. (As a temporary measure, you will find Marcus Aurelius' *Meditations* at <http://members.tripod.com/ptypes> and the complete text of Seneca's *Moral Letters* at <http://www.stoics.com/books.html>.) If the Robin Hard translation of the *Meditations* is not available, my personal preference for a substitute is the G. M. A. Grube translation from Hackett (see Bibliography).

Having your own copies will enable you to annotate them with your own notes, underline passages that you want to find easily, and make basic indexes at the back. The more you annotate your own copies of these books, the more useful you will find them, and the better acquainted you will be with their authors.

Lucius Annaeus Seneca (*c.*4 BC–AD 65) was tutor to the future Emperor Nero, and served as a senior minister in Nero's administration. He was implicated in a plot to assassinate Nero, and was forced to commit suicide. Seneca wrote several philosophical treatises, as well as the *Epistulae Morales ad Lucilium* ('Moral letters to Lucilius' = *Letters from a Stoic*). The *Letters* are clearly designed not just to inform his readers about Stoic philosophy, but also to persuade them to adopt a Stoic outlook and lifestyle.

Marcus Aurelius Antoninus (born AD 121) was emperor from 161 to 180. Whereas there can be absolutely no doubt that Seneca wrote for publication, Marcus' *Meditations* are notes written for his own private use. The book offers an intriguing insight into how Marcus strove to incorporate Stoic philosophy into a life which he felt was burdened by his responsibilities as emperor, but also shows that whatever our station in life, we can meet our obligations and face our difficulties with a calm commitment to seek the Stoic ideal.

SOME QUESTIONS ANSWERED

How long should I take to complete the course?

This very much depends upon the individual. There are six course papers to complete in total, and each will direct you to some required reading, as well as giving you short writing assignments and exercises. Some students will wish to devote a lot of time to their studies, in which case they will be able to complete each of the six course papers in a week, and finish the entire course in six weeks. Other students will wish to work at a substantially more relaxed pace, and will complete each paper roughly every two to three weeks. Momentum is important, and once you have started the course, it is strongly recommended that you maintain a strict and even pace until you have completed it.

How much will I have to read?

Each course paper will contain at least a few instructions for the reading of fairly small extracts from the set books. Each paper will conclude with a set of exercises, some of which will require further reading from the set books, or will include printed extracts from other sources. For those who wish to read more widely, I have included a fairly substantial Bibliography that also includes a list of recommended websites. There is a wealth of material on Stoicism and the Stoics available on the Internet, easily accessed via any search engine.

Will I have to compose written exercises?

Yes. Each course paper will conclude with an Exercises section that will ask you to prepare some written work. You will also be asked to maintain your own Journal in which you will keep notes about the texts you read as well as write brief exercises as directed by the course papers.

The best way to develop a familiarity and understanding of any body of ideas is to explain the material in writing, as if you are explaining it to someone else. In short, writing focuses the mind.

It will not matter if you have not done this sort of thing before, or if you are worried that you might not do it very well.

Will I be required to adopt certain beliefs or practices?

No. Almost by definition, philosophical ideas are to be discussed and debated, and if people think that any ideas are good ones, these ideas are defended and argued for rather than just 'believed'. This is the case with respect to ideas in Stoic philosophy. Your tutor will support you in your philosophical investigations (though at all times seeking to support Stoic ideas) no matter where they may lead you.

If, in doing this course, you adopt the Stoic outlook, this will happen because you have decided it is right, and *not* because anyone has coerced you.

Does Stoic philosophy offer a 'spiritual path' and must I believe in any sort of deity?

Many people would say that there is a spiritual path at the core of Stoicism. The fully confirmed Stoic, if they embrace the ideas of the ancient Stoic philosophers, will adopt a range of metaphysical and theological views concerning the nature of creation, providence and fate, the source of our rationality, and Deity.

In a more general sense, the notion of 'spiritual path', taken to mean 'way of life', 'outlook upon life', 'personal growth', 'personal healing', is in fact the very essence of Stoicism.

Some people accept the Stoic views on moral conduct, but reject the 'wilder' metaphysical and theological views. But you will not be *required* to adopt any particular beliefs.

Can you tell me something about the author?

This course was written by Keith Seddon, a founding trustee of the Stoic Foundation. He was born in London in 1956, and has always been dedicated to philosophy as a tool for personal development and enlightenment. He holds a BA in Humanities (University of Hertfordshire) and a PhD in Philosophy (University of London). Since 1985, after completing his doctorate thesis on the metaphysics of time, he has devoted himself to the philosophy of the ancients, including the philosophy of classical China and Greece, focusing on Taoism and Stoicism. Dr Seddon has worked as a lecturer and tutor in a variety of settings, and has worked as a correspondence tutor for several institutions, including Warnborough College, Ireland, where you will find a range of MA and PhD programmes, covering ancient philosophy, metaphysics, and philosophy of religion. He is married to Rev Dr Jocelyn Almond. They have co-authored books on the Tarot, and on ancient Egyptian religious rites. Together they founded, and currently run, the Lyceum of Isis Myrionymous, which offers correspondence courses within the Fellowship of Isis.

If you would like to contact Dr Seddon, please do so via his website:
http://www.btinternet.com/~k.h.s/stoic-foundation.htm
or by writing to him at:
BM Box 1129, London, WC1N 3XX, Great Britain.
You will find his programmes in post-graduate philosophy at Warnborough College, Ireland:
http://www.warnborough.ie

NOTE

1. Socrates was indicted by his enemies in 399 BC on charges of impiety and of corrupting the youth. The *Apology*, one of Plato's dialogues, is a reconstruction of Socrates' defence. (See *The Last Days of Socrates*, trans. Hugh Tredennich and Harold Tarrant, Penguin, 2003.) The jury sided against Socrates, and he was sentenced to death by poisoning. He was given the opportunity to escape and go into exile, but he thought it was wrong to disobey the law, even if it was applied unjustly (see Plato's dialogue *Crito* in *The Last Days of Socrates*). Socrates drank the poison and died.

1

GOOD, BAD AND INDIFFERENT

ZENO OF CITIUM

The Stoic school of philosophy was founded sometime around 300 BC in the ancient Greek city of Athens, by Zeno of Citium (which is in Cyprus).

Zeno was born in 335 BC. The ancient author Diogenes Laertius (third century AD), in his *On the Lives, Opinions, and Sayings of Eminent Philosophers*, tells us that Zeno was thirty years old when he was shipwrecked close to Athens. In the city, he sat down next to a bookseller who was reading aloud the second book of Xenophon's *Memorabilia* about Socrates. Zeno liked this so much that he asked the bookseller where he could meet with men like Socrates. As chance would have it, the Cynic philosopher Crates walked past at that very moment, and the bookseller pointed him out. 'Follow that man,' he said, and that is how Zeno came to be a student of Crates. There is another account (also related by Diogenes Laertius) which says that Zeno was already in Athens when he heard about the loss of his ship, upon which he gave up his career as a merchant and turned to philosophy, studying first with Crates, and after that with other philosophers.

Yet another story included in Diogenes' biography is that Zeno's father, Mnaseas, a merchant who frequently went to Athens, would bring back with him books about Socrates, which he gave to the young Zeno who, upon attaining adulthood, set off to study philosophy at Athens, having been inspired by the books. Diogenes Laertius cites ancient sources which say that Zeno consulted an oracle to find out what he should do to live the best life, and the god's reply was that he should 'take on the complexion of the dead', which Zeno understood to mean that he should study the writings of the ancient philosophers.

These biographical details are too uncertain for us to accept with any degree of confidence, but what we can be sure of is that Zeno came to Athens and studied with a number of philosophers, including Crates, before establishing his own school.

Zeno's followers were called Zenoians at first, but because Zeno taught his classes in the painted colonnade (*poikilê stoa*) – so-called because it was decorated with murals by Polygnotus and other fifth-century artists – located at the north-eastern side of Athens' central *agora* (marketplace), they soon came to be known as 'the men from the Stoa', or Stoics. He was active until his death in 263 BC.

None of Zeno's works survive, though Diogenes Laertius records their titles, including *Of Life According to Nature, Of Emotions, Of Duty, The Republic, Of Greek Education*, and *Ethics*. Zeno's teaching, both oral and written (though not unmodified by his successors) established and inspired what many have deemed was the most successful of the Hellenistic schools. In the ancient world, Marcus Aurelius is often considered to be the last of the Stoics, which means that the Stoic school lasted for almost five centuries. Stoic strands can be seen in the history of thought down through the ages, from its influence on early Christian thought, to Humanist thought in our own age, whose beliefs in the fellowship of all people and the primacy of reason were first woven into Stoic doctrine over two thousand two hundred years ago by Zeno of Citium.

WHAT IS GOOD?

Is there anything that *really has value*? Is there something that *really ought to be pursued*? On our quest for well-being, on our search to find the best way to live, at what should we aim?

What should we value, and what should we do to fully flourish? What is of ultimate importance? In the midst of uncertainties of all sorts, when people can cheat us, when illness can strike without warning, when life is in essence precarious, we may wonder whether aiming to live well and to fully flourish makes any sense at all.

Much of the foundation that Stoic ethics rests on was laid down many years before Zeno even thought of taking up his studies. In Plato's dialogue, *Euthydemus*, written about one hundred years before Zeno opened his school, we find a discussion of what promotes happiness. Socrates, the narrator of these extracts, is conversing with the young man Clinias, son of Axiochus:

> And now, O son of Axiochus, let me put a question to you: Do not all men desire happiness? And yet, perhaps, this is one of those ridiculous questions which I am afraid to ask, and which ought not to be asked by a sensible man: for what human being is there who does not desire happiness?
> There is no one, said Clinias, who does not.
> Well, then, I said, since we all of us desire happiness, how can we be happy? – that is the next question. Shall we not be happy if we have many good things? And this, perhaps, is even a more simple question than the first, for there can be no doubt of the answer.
> He assented.
> And what things do we esteem good? No solemn sage is required to tell us this, which may be easily answered; for every one will say that wealth is a good.
> Certainly, he said.

And are not health and beauty goods, and other personal gifts?

He agreed.

Now, can there be any doubt that good birth, and power, and honours in one's own land, are goods?

He assented.

And what other goods are there? I said. What do you say of temperance, justice, courage: do you not verily and indeed think, Clinias, that we shall be more right in ranking them as goods than in not ranking them as goods? For a dispute might possibly arise about this. What then do you say?

They are goods, said Clinias.

Very well, I said; and in what company shall we find a place for wisdom – among the goods or not?

Among the goods.

(Plato, *Euthydemus* 278e–279c, trans. Jowett)

IN YOUR JOURNAL.[1] Make a list of all the goods that Socrates identifies. There are two distinct types of goods, here, (a) the ones that Socrates mentions first, and (b) the ones he mentions last. Try to think of headings for the two types of goods.

The second group is easier to identify and name: this group of goods consists of *temperance* (i.e., self-restraint), *justice*, *courage*, and *wisdom*. These could be named as 'personal qualities', 'spiritual qualities', 'parts of one's character', or something like that. They can also be called the *virtues*, which is what the ancients called them. For the Stoics, as this course will make clear, the virtues are of key significance to living well.

The first group of goods includes wealth, beauty, 'personal gifts' (perhaps intended to cover features such as strength, good eyesight, intelligence, a good voice, and so on), 'good birth' (of significantly less importance for us today), power and honours. But what shall we name them collectively? Just 'Goods', perhaps? Or 'Goods that practically everyone pursues', or 'What most people want'? Maybe even 'What I would like to have myself'! Or 'Goods that bring happiness'.

A bit later, Socrates continues:

> You remember, I said, our making the admission that we should be happy and fortunate if many good things were present with us?
>
> He assented.
>
> And should we be happy by reason of the presence of good things, if they profited us not, or if they profited us?
>
> If they profited us, he said.
>
> And would they profit us, if we only had them and did not use them? For example, if we had a great deal of food and did not eat, or a great deal of drink and did not drink, should we be profited?
>
> Certainly not, he said.
>
> Or would an artisan, who had all the implements necessary for his work, and did not use them, be any the better for the possession of all that he ought to possess? For example, would a carpenter be any the better for having all his tools and plenty of wood, if he never worked?
>
> Certainly not, he said.
>
> And if a person had wealth and all the goods of which we were just now speaking, and did not use them, would he be happy because he possessed them?
>
> No indeed, Socrates.
>
> Then, I said, a man who would be happy must not only have the good things, but he must also use them; there is no advantage in merely having them?
>
> True.

Well, Clinias, but if you have the use as well as the possession of good things, is that sufficient to confer happiness?

Yes, in my opinion.

And may a person use them either rightly or wrongly?

He must use them rightly.

That is quite true, I said. And the wrong use of a thing is far worse than the non-use; for the one is an evil, and the other is neither a good nor an evil. You admit that?

He assented.

(Plato, *Euthydemus* 280b–281a, trans. Jowett)

[Note: Benjamin Jowett's translation made in the nineteenth century translated the Greek term *ôphelimos* as 'profitable'. For us, the notion of 'profit' is pretty much confined to business and making money, which creates an emphasis that Plato, and Jowett, did not intend. *Ôphelimos* means helpful, useful, advantageous, beneficial. Try swapping Jowett's 'profit' and 'profited' for 'benefit' and 'benefited', and the sentences may seem less stilted.]

> IN YOUR JOURNAL. Explain why, according to Socrates, merely having possession of good things is not sufficient to confer happiness.
>
> What does Clinias conclude is sufficient for happiness?

Clinias concludes that *using* the good things that one possesses, and using them *well* or *properly* ('rightly') is sufficient to confer happiness. Socrates makes the following conclusion:

Then, I said, Clinias, the sum of the matter appears to be that the goods of which we spoke before are not to be regarded as goods in themselves, but the degree of good and evil in them depends on whether they are or are not under the guidance of knowledge: under the guidance of ignorance, they are greater evils than their opposites, inasmuch as they are more able to minister to the evil principle which rules them; and when under the guidance of wisdom and virtue, they are greater goods: but in themselves are nothing?

That, he said, appears to be certain.

What then, I said, is the result of all this? Is not this the result — that other things are neither good nor bad, and that wisdom is good, and ignorance is evil?

He assented.

(Plato, *Euthydemus* 281d–e, trans. Jowett, modified)

Socrates says that for conventional goods, such as wealth, health and power, to truly benefit their possessor, they must be used properly, 'under the guidance of wisdom and virtue'. That is, the first sort of goods identified in the first extract above can confer benefit only if the agent also possesses the second sort of goods, the *virtues*, or qualities of character. What we see is that for benefit to result, the virtues have a job of work to do in guiding our actions.

THE INDIFFERENTS

The Stoics would later agree with Socrates when he says that conventional goods are 'in themselves nothing', that they are 'neither good nor bad'. Although popularly conceived of as 'good', it is clear to see that wealth, for example, can as easily be used to cause harm as it can be used to produce benefit. Wealth may be used by its possessor to harm others, or even themselves (as would be the case for someone who ended up using their wealth to obtain illegal drugs resulting in damage to their health or even death – or in their being caught and sent to prison). Clearly, wealth cannot be considered in *itself* as good. What is *really good* lies in those qualities of character, the virtues of temperance, justice, courage and wisdom, through whose application the conventional 'goods' may be used to benefit the agent, as well as, often, other people too.

The Stoics refer to the conventional 'goods', including wealth and health, as the *indifferents*, because such 'goods' are indifferent with respect to being good or bad. They fall into neither category. The conventional 'goods' are also indifferent with respect to our really needing them to achieve true well-being and for its being possible for us to flourish. This does not mean that we should ourselves be indifferent towards the indifferents, as we will see later. Such things as food and shelter, and possibly a few other things, are clearly needed for living at all. In saying that these things are indifferent, the Stoics do not mean that we can actually live entirely without them. In some way they are needed and even desired, but however we come to understand this, the Stoics insist that the indifferent things are not in themselves good or bad.

THE VIRTUES

For the Stoics then, of supreme importance is the development of character: what matters more than anything is that we should in all circumstances, and at all times, act virtuously, which means that when it is appropriate we must act with self-restraint, we must be just towards others, we must face difficult or painful circumstances with courage, and we must choose our activities and carry them out wisely. The Stoics maintain that merely in doing this, if we can do this, we will live well, we will be happy. Nothing else is required for us to flourish fully.

For many, if not for all, changing our attitude towards the 'indifferents', the conventional 'goods' that are not really good at all, is very difficult. For many people, their material 'goods' are of ultimate importance: they quite literally devote their lives to acquiring and maintaining these indifferent things. We live in a society that says loudly and persistently, in so many ways, that material goods are of extreme importance. So many people expend their efforts upon the pursuit of, not what they need, but what they have been convinced they want. Sadly, this is a futile endeavour, for no matter how much is obtained, it is inevitable that there is always more to acquire, more to want. Clearly there is some sort of folly at work here. Indeed, the Stoics describe people who are not Stoic sages, as fools.

> **Read Seneca, *Letters from a Stoic*, Letter 9, from 'The wise man, nevertheless...' (halfway down page 52) to the end (= *Moral Letters* 9.18–22).**

Here is the story of the philosopher Stilpo,[2] who was head of the Megarian school. He lived too early to be a Stoic, and was in fact one of Zeno's teachers. Very few people have the misfortune to lose everything, as Stilpo did when Demetrius' forces captured and sacked his home town. Starting out as students who wish to 'make progress' towards leading the philosophic life, the idea that someone should be able to retain their equanimity and poise, and truly remain a 'happy man' amid such destruction and loss, sounds preposterous.

Stilpo did not regard as valuable anything that could be taken away from him. These things are not 'in our power', not 'in our control' as the Stoics say, and they are the indifferent things. Stilpo's happiness is dependent only upon possession of the 'valuables' that he still has with him, and these are the virtues, 'the qualities of a just, a good and an enlightened character'.

This does not mean that Stilpo did not care for his wife and children, and for his material possessions. While it was his lot to have them, he cared for them as a man of good character should. To get a better grip on this we can make a distinction using terms that the ancient Stoics did not actually employ. We need to distinguish between our interests and projects on the one hand, and the *way* we carry on the business of pursuing our interests and furthering our projects on the other. Everything that we engage in in daily life will further some project which in turn satisfies some interest we have. Interests would include earning an income, gaining an education, staying healthy, raising children, etc., etc. A project is some activity we perform which furthers an interest, such as taking a course at a local college, or taking up a new diet. Notice that interests and projects concern indifferent things (with the singular and unique exception of our interest to perfect our characters and thereby to fully flourish and live happily). But the *way* we carry out our projects – noting that the way we act in pursuit of something is entirely distinct from the project itself – concerns our capacity to act virtuously, to act in ways characteristic of the person who has perfected their character. *This*, say the Stoics, is what is good or bad, and this is what is of supreme importance.

Once we adopt this view of how we engage in our affairs, we can see that when disaster strikes, whether in small ways as frustrating setbacks, or as complete calamities, it is our interests and projects that are harmed. As agents endeavouring to perfect our characters, to act in ways that are proper for rational human beings, *we have not been harmed*. Seen in this way, agents – that is, rational, sentient and self-conscious creatures, capable of deciding what to do and the means of doing it – are not the sort of thing that *can* be harmed. Stilpo could well have said: 'All my interests and projects have ended today. My interests to be a good husband and a good father have been brought to an end – I can no longer pursue them. So too for all my other activities. I can no longer be a good friend to my neighbours, for all my neighbours have been slain.'

However, he could have continued: 'But my wife and children, my neighbours and all my possessions, were never really mine to begin with. Fate entrusted them to me for a time, and now they have been taken back. What is truly my own, my capacities to act wisely and with self-restraint, to be just and courageous, I still have, and these truly good things I will deploy upon my new interests and projects. I will be a good friend to all whom I meet; I will deal fairly with people – in short, I will carry on as before, doing my best to perfect my character and to be a good man.'

Stilpo and Zeno, and the Stoics who came after them, declare that well-being and happiness are to be found not in what we have as material possessions, but what we have in terms of good characters, whose qualities we deploy upon circumstances and situations that we encounter in the course of living. These circumstances and situations are ultimately beyond our control, from an eyelash falling in our eye, to the death of a loved one. Even to focus on this fully and honestly can be unsettling and disturbing, but doing this, and recognising the truth of how things really are, is an important step towards the peace and equanimity that are sought by those striving for enlightenment.

MARCUS AURELIUS ON MISFORTUNE AND INDIFFERENT THINGS

There is very little doubt that Seneca wrote for publication, and his writings have the polished finish of carefully crafted essays. Marcus Aurelius, however, almost certainly did *not* intend his writings to be published. What we read in the *Meditations* constitutes notes and jottings put down by the author as his own private repository of thoughts and explorations. The 'chapters' in the 'books' veer from topic to topic, themes are picked up and dropped, then picked up again, seemingly at random.

Unlike Seneca, Marcus is not preaching or teaching, he is merely making notes. But in reading both authors, we get a sense of how these thinkers tried to incorporate Stoic ideals into their daily lives.

If you wish, as you progress through the course, please use your Journal to write down your own 'Stoic Notes', to build your own personal repository of thoughts and explorations.

Marcus' *Meditations* are divided into 'books', each of which is comprised of several 'chapters'. Thus, a reference to the *Meditations* given as 9.4, means 'chapter' 4 of 'book' 9. In the Wordsworth edition (the one recommended for this course), an asterisk (*) indicates that a note by the editor will be found in the 'Notes' section that follows immediately upon Marcus' text. Please read these notes, as they are helpful.

When Marcus addresses the reader as 'you' he means *himself*. But in many instances the sense and the force of Marcus' meaning is preserved if we suppose that he is addressing *us*. In addressing himself, Marcus was addressing someone who sought to live as a Stoic, and much of what he says is directly applicable to us.

> 📖 **Read Marcus Aurelius, *Meditations*, sections 4.49 on dealing with misfortunes; 5.36 on how to aid those who have suffered a loss; 8.1 on what is truly good; and 11.16 about indifferent things.**

These readings may come across as somewhat obscure or rather puzzling, but hopefully not wholly so. Marcus is writing to remind himself of what he already knows, and as you become better acquainted with Stoic ideas, you will find that the *Meditations* make more sense than they did at first. You will find also that they are not only a source for Stoic ideas, but are also a source of inspiration for students on the Stoic path.

EXERCISES

1. Use your Journal to write up a record of your daily affairs, and try to identify your interests and projects. Try to identify the most basic interests that your life is devoted to, such as being a spouse, being a parent, being an employer or employee; then try to identify some of the projects that you engage in to further your interests. Write how well or how badly any of your projects are going, and write up how you dealt with the situations you face. As the days pass, try to be conscious on an hour-by-hour basis of which project you are engaged on, and try to be aware of the distinction between *what* you are doing from the *way* you do it.

Pay attention in particular to the way you handle setbacks or frustrations. If anything goes badly, try to be aware that you have not in yourself been harmed, though possibly your *project* has.

Send to your tutor your work on identifying your interests and projects, as well as two or three Journal entries, focusing on those that you feel can demonstrate your capacity to distinguish harm to yourself from harm to your project.

2. Read Letter 91 from *Letters from a Stoic* (pp. 177–83). Seneca takes the news from his friend Liberalis about the destruction of the city of Lyons by fire as a cue for writing a letter to Lucilius about how we should face misfortune and mortality generally. From what you have learned from this paper and from Seneca's writing, compose an imaginary dialogue between Liberalis and Stilpo, showing how Stilpo would have advised Liberalis as they stand in the smouldering ruins of the city. If you wish, allow that Stilpo can draw on points that Seneca employs himself in this letter.

NOTES

1. Please find a suitable notebook to use as your Journal, or use loose leaves which you can keep in a binder. You will use your Journal for writing up a variety of tasks, including brief exercises in the course of reading the papers, longer exercises at the conclusion of each paper, and other tasks.
2. Seneca spells the name 'Stilpo' with a 'b'.

2

WHAT IS IN OUR POWER

As you carry on with your work on the course, please continue to write up in your Journal accounts of your daily experiences, explaining in as much detail as you like the things that occur, and detailing your thoughts and reactions. As you have been doing already, identify your interests and projects, and try to be aware of the distinction between *what* you are doing from the *way* you do it.

In this paper we will look more closely at the distinction between our interests and projects on the one hand, and ourselves as agents who engage in projects on the other. To start, we will look at the contribution of the Stoic teacher Epictetus and what he says about the nature of human agency and what is 'in our power' as agents who engage in projects.

EPICTETUS

Apart from the writings of Seneca and Marcus Aurelius, the only other ancient work by a Stoic philosopher to have survived into our own era is that of Epictetus (*c.* AD 55–*c.*135). (The writings of other ancient Stoics survive only as fragments and summaries in later works. The early Stoic Chrysippus, for instance, is known to have been a prolific author, yet unfortunately none of his writings has survived – we have to rely on Cicero and other authors for summaries and quotations.) However, the writings we refer to as

Epictetus', the *Discourses* and the *Handbook*, were not actually written by Epictetus himself: they were written by his pupil Flavius Arrian who attended his lectures. (A similar situation arose with some of the writings of the philosopher Ludwig Wittgenstein in the twentieth century. The *Blue and Brown Books* are popularly referred to as 'by Wittgenstein', though these texts were in fact compiled by Wittgenstein's students from notes taken down during his lectures.)

Epictetus would have been a boy of about ten at the time Emperor Nero forced Seneca to commit suicide. He was born in Hierapolis in Phrygia (now central Turkey), and somehow he came to Rome where he was a slave of Epaphroditus who was a freedman, having himself earlier been a slave of Nero. At some point Epictetus was freed, and it is known that he studied with the Stoic teacher Musonius Rufus. Epictetus opened his own Stoic school in Rome but, along with all the other philosophers in the city, was banished by the Emperor Domitian sometime around AD 89. He went to Nicopolis in north-western Greece and opened a new school there which acquired a good reputation, attracting many upper-class Romans including his student Flavius Arrian who would compose the *Discourses* and the *Handbook*, and who later would serve in public office under the Emperor Hadrian and make his mark as a respected historian. (Much of his writing survives.)

Marcus Aurelius, the future Emperor and Stoic philosopher, would have been a boy in his teens at the time Epictetus died. It was Marcus' tutor, Quintus Junius Rusticus, who introduced him to Epictetus' *Discourses*, which resulted in Marcus' turning from rhetoric to philosophy as his main area of interest for study.

Epictetus' *Discourses* appear to record the exchanges between Epictetus and his students after formal teaching had concluded for the day. It is highly likely that Epictetus would have presented lectures on all the major Stoic philosophers from Zeno onwards, at which their works would have been examined in detail, but this aspect of Epictetus' teaching is not recorded by Arrian. What we have, then, are intimate and earnest discussions in which Epictetus aims to make his students consider carefully what the philosophic life consists in and how to live it oneself. He discusses a wide range of topics, from friendship to illness, from fear to poverty, on how to acquire and maintain tranquillity, and why we should not be angry with other people.

WHAT IS 'IN OUR POWER'

One of Epictetus' main themes is that of what is 'in our power', and our having an understanding of this concept will advance us well along the path towards the philosophic life as the Stoics conceived it.

> There are things which are within our power, and there are things which are beyond our power. Within our power are opinion, aim, desire, aversion, and, in a word, whatever affairs are our own. Beyond our power are body, property, reputation, office, and, in one word, whatever are not properly our own affairs.
> (Epictetus, *Enchiridion* 1, trans. Higginson 1890, 215)[1]

What does Epictetus mean by 'whatever affairs are our own' and 'whatever are not properly our own affairs'? And how can this help us make progress as Stoics? Should we not regard *everything* that happens to us, *everything* we concern ourselves with, as 'our own affairs'?

This opening and rather perplexing paragraph of the *Handbook* is thankfully expanded upon at some length in the *Discourses*:

> What is it, then, that makes a man free and independent? For neither riches, nor consulship, nor the command of

provinces nor of kingdoms, can make him so; but something else must be found. What is it that keeps any one from being hindered and restrained in penmanship, for instance? 'The science of penmanship.' In music? 'The science of music.' Therefore in life too, it must be the science of living. As you have heard it in general, then, consider it likewise in particulars. Is it possible for him to be unrestrained who desires any of those things that are within the power of others? 'No.' Can he avoid being hindered? 'No.' Therefore neither can he be free. Consider, then, whether we have nothing or everything in our own sole power, – or whether some things are in our own power and some in that of others. 'What do you mean?' When you would have your body perfect, is it in your own power, or is it not? 'It is not.' When you would be healthy? 'It is not.' When you would be handsome? 'It is not.' When you would live or die? 'It is not.' Body then is not our own; but is subject to everything that proves stronger than itself. 'Agreed.' Well; is it in your own power to have an estate when you please, and such a one as you please? 'No.' Slaves? 'No.' Clothes? 'No.' A house? 'No.' Horses? 'Indeed, none of these.' Well, if you desire ever so earnestly to have your children live, or your wife, or your brother, or your friends, is it in your own power? 'No, it is not.'

Will you then say that there is *nothing* independent, which is in your own power alone, and unalienable? See if you have anything of this sort. 'I do not know.' But consider it thus: can any one make you assent to a falsehood? 'No one.' In the matter of assent, then, you are unrestrained and unhindered. 'Agreed'. Well, and can anyone compel you to exert your aims towards what you do not like? 'He can. For when he threatens me with death, or fetters, he thus compels me.' If, then, you were to despise dying or being fettered, would you any longer regard him? 'No.' Is despising death, then, an action in our power, or is it not? 'It is.' Is it therefore in your power also to exert your aims towards anything, or is it not? 'Agreed that it is. But in whose power is my avoiding anything?' This, too, is in your own. 'What then if, when I am exerting myself to walk, any one should restrain me?' What part of you can he restrain? Can he restrain your assent? 'No, but my body.' Ay, as he may a stone. 'Be it so. But still I cease to walk.' And who claimed that walking was one of the actions that cannot be restrained? For I only said that your exerting yourself towards it could not be restrained. But whenever the body and its assistance are essential, you have already heard that nothing is in your power. 'Be this, too, agreed.' And can any one compel you to desire against your will? 'No one.' Or to propose, or intend, or, in short, not to be beguiled by the appearances of things? 'Nor this. But when I desire anything, he can restrain me from obtaining what I desire.' If you desire anything that is truly within your reach, and that cannot be restrained, how can he restrain you? 'By no means.' And pray who claims that he who longs for what depends on another will be free from restraint?

'May I not long for health, then?' By no means; nor for anything else that depends on another; for what is not in your own power, either to procure or to preserve when you will, *that* belongs to another. Keep off not only your hands from it, but even more than these, your desires. Otherwise you have given yourself up as a slave; you have put your neck under the yoke, if you admire any of the things which are not your own, but which are subject and mortal, to whichever of them soever you are attached. 'Is not my hand my own?' It is a part of you, but it is by nature clay, liable to restraint, to compulsion; a slave to everything stronger than itself. And why do I say, your hand? You ought to hold your whole body but as a useful ass, with a pack-saddle on, so long as may be, so long as it is allowed you. But if there should come a military conscription, and a soldier should lay hold on it, let it go. Do not resist, or murmur; otherwise you will be first beaten and lose the ass after all. And since you are thus to regard even the body itself, think what remains to do concerning things to be provided for the sake of the body. If that be an ass, the rest are but bridles, pack-saddles, shoes, oats, hay for him. Let these go too. Quit them yet more easily and expeditiously. And when you are thus prepared and trained to distinguish what belongs to others from your own; what is liable to restraint from what is not; to esteem the one your own property, but not the other; to keep your desire, to keep your aversion, carefully regulated by this point, – whom have you any longer to fear? 'No one.' For about what should you be afraid, – about what is your own, in which consists the essence of good and evil? And who has any power over *this*? Who can take it away?

(Epictetus, *Discourses* 4.1.62–82, trans. Higginson 1890, 128–31)

IN YOUR JOURNAL. From the first paragraph of the extract above, identify the specific items that Epictetus says are not in our power. Do you agree with him? What sorts of response might someone make to Epictetus?

Epictetus offers a range of things that are not in our power. Our bodies, he says, are not in our power: specifically, whether we have 'perfect' bodies, whether they are healthy or handsome, nor whether they go on living or not. 'Body then is not our own.' He goes on to identify a range of external goods that are not in our power: having an estate, or having just such a one as we please, slaves (not applicable to us in our modern setting), clothes, a house, and horses (perhaps we could substitute 'car' for 'horses'). Epictetus concludes the paragraph by mentioning *other people's* bodies: no matter how earnestly we desire it, it is not in our power as to whether our children live, nor our spouses, brothers and sisters, nor our friends.

At first sight, this could appear as an awfully gloomy picture. Everything around us, including even our own bodies, Epictetus says, are entirely beyond our power to control. Yet is this wholly correct? The thought that my health is *entirely* beyond my control seems mistaken. It is up to me to eat a healthy diet, and it is up to me to avoid dangers of various sorts. If I feel unwell, I may call in the doctor. As with any of my possessions, I may take a wide variety of measures to look after my body properly.

Epictetus would not disagree with this. He would say that everyone has a responsibility to care for their own bodies, and those who are striving for wisdom especially so. But he would reply that the 'power' we have to care for our bodies is partial and limited, no matter how much care we take. If we feel ill, the responsible course of action is to go to the doctor; but whether we become ill or not in the first place – even allowing for our taking every precaution to steer clear of infectious people, contaminated food and toxic sites – is not in our power. And having arrived at the doctor's – even allowing that we took every precaution to find a good doctor – it is not in our power as to whether we get even a correct diagnosis, let alone an effective treatment. And most certainly, it is not in our power as to whether we were born handsome, or disabled – and like it or not, we have absolutely no power as to whether we number among the very few who have the misfortune to suffer a sudden and fatal brain haemorrhage, nor whether we will perish in a moment should an asteroid from outer space smash into the earth.

Whatever steps we take to attain what we desire, or to avoid what we do not want, we can provide ourselves with no *guarantee* that we will meet with success. Certainly it is sensible and rational to try our best. But whether we get what we know to be sensible, is not in our power. Epictetus then, and the Stoics generally, place the emphasis not on *getting* what we want, but on *trying* to get what is sensible.

If we invest all our hopes in getting what we desire, we are likely to be disappointed a great deal of the time. But if we invest our hope instead in trying our best – so long as we have trained ourselves to be experts in this skill – we will never be disappointed.

> **IN YOUR JOURNAL. Read again the second paragraph of the extract above, and write down the items that Epictetus says *are* in our power.**

There are two types of item here. One is our 'assenting' to things. This is our capacity to hold that something is true or false. This is always and wholly in our power. How we judge things is our own affair. Even when we are the victims of deceit, how we eventually judge some matter is entirely within our own control (though the guarantee here does not extend to our judgements always being right).

We may judge that '2 + 2 = 4', for example. Our capacity to hold that this is the case can never be taken from us. Even if a cruel torturer should attempt to force us to believe that '2 + 2 = 5', he must fail. Even if under the influence of extreme pain we should cry out, 'Yes! Two plus two equals five!' we would be lying, and we would know ourselves to be lying. Our uttering the sentence does not mean that someone else has gained power over our own capacity to make judgements. Epictetus points out that our capacity to judge death as nothing to fear (to 'despise' death) is within our own power. He calls this an 'action', and we can allow that forming judgements is a special sort of acting. It is certainly a sort of 'doing something'.

The other item that Epictetus identifies as being in our power is our capacity to 'exert our aim' towards something, and this is more readily understood as the capacity to *intend to act* in some particular way. Epictetus' example is that of walking. That I may walk is not entirely in my power: I may be locked in a cupboard, my legs might be restrained, I may have been injected with some paralysing agent on the part of a mad scientist. Any of these restraints will prevent my walking. Even so, my *intending* to walk, conceived of as my capacity to *wish* to walk, and my capacity to *try* to walk, is entirely in my power. As Epictetus says, my 'exerting' myself 'towards' walking cannot be restrained.

Thus, our body and the things in the world external to our bodies are not (entirely) in our power. But things that are internal, our thoughts, judgements (about what to pursue and what to avoid, and how matters stand), and intentions about how we would like to act, and what we would like to attempt, *are* (entirely) in our power.

ACTING 'WITH RESERVATION'

Once we realise that things that happen in the world, including the way other people act, are not wholly in our power, we come into possession of a wonderful gift, for now we can engage in our affairs with a sort of serenity, a newfound peace of mind and an empowering confidence. We do this by acting 'with reservation'. Seneca says:

> The safest policy is rarely to tempt [Fortune], though to keep her always in mind and to trust her in nothing. Thus: 'I shall sail unless something happens'; and 'I shall become praetor unless something prevents me', and 'My business will be successful unless something interferes.' That is why we say that nothing happens to a wise man against his expectation.
> (*On Tranquillity of Mind* 13.2–3, trans. Costa 1997, 51–2)

Two further extracts illustrate the same approach:

> They [the Stoics] say that nothing happens to the good man which is contrary to his inclination (*orexis*) or his impulse or his intention, on account of the fact that he does everything of this kind with a reservation (*hupexhairesis*), and nothing which he would not want can happen unexpectedly.
>
> (Stobaeus 2.115.5–9, trans. Donini, Inwood and Donini 1999, 737)

> The wise man sets about every action with reservation: 'if nothing happens which might stop him'. For this reason we say that he always succeeds and that nothing unexpected happens to him: because within himself he considers the possibility that something will get in the way and prevent what he is proposing to do.
>
> (Seneca, *On Benefits* 4.34.4, trans. Donini, Inwood and Donini 1999, 737)

Marcus Aurelius uses the term *hupexhairesis* ('with reservation') five times in the *Meditations*, at 4.1, 5.20, 6.50, 8.41 and 11.37.

📖 **Read Marcus Aurelius, *Meditations* 4.1.**

This is a fairly technical passage, and we need to define some of Marcus' expressions. 'Ruling power' in the first sentence is best thought of as our power of agency, that aspect of ourselves which thinks and feels and decides what to do. The Stoics believed that there is a proper way for us to use our capacity for agency when dealing with affairs in the world which they described as 'living according to nature'. We will explore this idea in the next paper. 'Primary objects' means the preferred indifferents (which we discussed in Paper 1), so in the first part of this paragraph, Marcus says that the proper way for us to engage with the world is to pursue the preferred indifferents 'with reservation'. And if we fail to get what we had aimed for, like a burning fire that 'masters' (i.e. burns) everything that falls into it, we will immediately turn ourselves in a creative and responsible way to the new situation we are in. Indeed, in our capacity to deal with new developments, especially after a disappointment or failure, we should be not like a 'little lamp' but like a 'blazing fire'.

> **Read Marcus Aurelius, *Meditations* 5.20 and 6.50.**

When we are faced with obstructive or even bad people who block our plans, we should recognise that 'they are not hindrances to [our] impulses or [our] disposition' – they cannot prevent us from attempting to do what is both sensible and right. We are not like Marcus who, as emperor, had absolute authority over everyone, though in family life, and in the business world, we may exercise a certain degree of authority over others; and when it is appropriate we should 'try to persuade' bad people into better behaviour. But if the worst happens, and our actions are thwarted we should retain our equanimity and 'refuse to yield to distress'. What we had intended to do was of course done 'with reservation', and 'was not unconditional' as our translation puts it. To always require success is to aim at the impossible. But in aiming to do what is right and sensible 'with reservation' we have in merely trying met with complete success.

When we face a setback we must 'display another virtue' – certainly remaining calm and patient is important, and if we do that we are likely to be able to make a more intelligent reassessment of the situation. We will have to decide whether there is any hope of pursuing our aim in some other way, or whether we must abandon it. And as Stoics, so long as we have deliberated intelligently, abandoning some action is for us a success, for all we are doing is rationally turning away from just one particular scheme in order to devote ourselves to another one that we believe to be more worthy of our 'ruling power'.

In short, what the Stoic is able to do is pick up new roles and new aims, as circumstances require, without getting frustrated and angry. 'I was driving along, and my car broke down!' So now you must stop being a driver and become someone who sorts out a broken-down car. 'The bank manager refused to make the loan!' So now your plans must change. 'But I was going to start my own business!' And now you must think again; and does getting upset really help matters? 'But the stupid manager didn't understand my business plan!' And who told you that you were destined to have a highly intelligent bank manager?

> 📖 **Read Marcus Aurelius, *Meditations* 2.5, 2.16 and 2.17.**

EXERCISES

1. In your Journal write up accounts of your daily affairs and identify the things that are in your power and the things that are not in your power. For example, you might write: 'Went shopping. In my power: the decision to do this. Not in my power: getting there (the car might have broken down – it didn't, but it might have); finding the shop open (there might have been a fire – there wasn't, but there might have been); finding the goods I wanted ... '

Maintain a record for as long as you like, but do this for a minimum of one week. Do not worry that you will be including everyday, trivial events.

Be sure to include any occasion when things *did go wrong*. Write down your *reactions* to setbacks and disappointments. You might write something like: 'Went shopping. In my power: the decision to do this. Not in my power: finding the shop was shut! In my power: getting annoyed at this, so decided not to!'

Be aware that even though external circumstances may urge a particular reaction – such as becoming annoyed that the shop was shut – it is nevertheless entirely within your power as to whether you actually get annoyed.

2. Identify three or four incidents (recent or long past, as you please) in which your aim to have something happen was thwarted, and which you consider serve as good examples of how you can get upset about things. Write brief accounts of exactly what happened and how you felt. With respect to each situation, imagine that you had had the good fortune to meet with a Stoic who encourages you to act 'with reservation'. Write down the sorts of thing that they would have said to you.

Do you think such a conversation would have helped you to cope better?

Identify three or four activities you have planned for the next week or two. Write down how you will attempt to engage in your activities 'with reservation'. Once you have performed these tasks write down how well or badly they went. Were you successful at acting 'with reservation'? Did you detect any benefit from making the attempt?

3. While you are working on the first two exercises, at any convenient moment when you have some free time, read Letters 7 and 8 from Seneca's *Letters from a Stoic* (pp. 41–7).

Seneca suggests that associating with large numbers of people is harmful, that he has gone home more cruel and less humane through having had contact with human beings. Even someone with a moral character such as that possessed by Socrates, Cato or Laelius can have their principles shaken by 'a multitude of people different from himself' (these three figures are described in the Index to *Letters from a Stoic*).

Our moral characters are easily undermined, he suggests, our internal peace is easily unsettled, the virtues we are working to secure are in fact frail and fragile, easily disturbed by displays of vice in those around us.

How happy are you to accept Seneca's picture?

It cannot be denied that in setting out on our quest for inner peace, as the ancient Stoics conceived it, we are immediately separating ourselves from the bulk of humanity, the majority of which, as Seneca points out, would entirely fail to grasp the value or significance of the project we have set ourselves.

Some students on this course will no doubt have friends and relatives who are sympathetic to and even interested in what you are doing. But others, alas, to be sure, will have been faced with incomprehension, bafflement, and even hostility or ridicule when you have tried to explain your interest in Stoic philosophy. For some students, this may be quite unsettling. It is entirely possible that in quite a short space of time, you have begun to change your outlook, to value things differently, to re-order your interests and priorities. From your point of view, these changes are important and significant; indeed, life may be taking on a wholly new complexion. But your friends and relatives, in noticing these changes, may be plain bemused, or worse, they may be downright hostile to your new 'philosophic life'.

For still others, this business of seeing things differently, of questioning the value and importance of material goods, may have been for you quite natural, and is already a part of your personality. Maybe you have felt separated from 'the crowd' for a long time, and that the lessons of Stoic philosophy do not really teach you anything new, but rather confirm and support what you have always thought all along.

3a. If you wish, please make a response to the idea that the philosopher is different from other people, and what this means for you personally.

3b. Is Seneca right when he says 'you must inevitably either hate or imitate the world at large'? (*Letters from a Stoic*, p. 43 = *Moral Letters* 7.7)

3c. Why does Seneca say that 'thatch makes a person just as good a roof as gold does'? (*Letters from a Stoic*, p. 46 = *Moral Letters* 8.5)

NOTE

1. *'Handbook'*, *'Enchiridion'*, *'Encheiridion'*, and *'Manual'* all refer to the same work.

3

'LIVE SIMPLY' AND 'LIVE ACCORDING TO NATURE'

As you write in your Journal and as you work at the exercises set for you, as you take the first steps as one 'making progress' in Stoic philosophy, it is possible that you may wonder where all this effort is leading. 'I have tried to act "with reservation", and I understand that everything external to my own will is "not in my power" – yet when I meet with obstacles, or when my projects founder, I cannot help but get upset, and if I think someone is to blame, I still get angry with them! I understand why the Stoics called the conventional goods "indifferents", yet I spend my time pursuing them, as I ever did, thinking them to be no less valuable, no less *good*, than before I started this course! Where is the peace of mind, the happiness and tranquillity that philosophy promises? If I try to perfect my character, if I strive to live by the virtues, as the Stoics urge, what's in it *for me?*'

One of Epictetus' interlocutors asks this very question – why *should* someone endeavour to do what is right?

> 'What does he gain by doing right?'
> What does a man gain [replies Epictetus] who writes Dio's name correctly? The gain of writing.
> 'Is there no further reward?'

> Do you look for any greater reward for a good man than to do what is noble and right?
>
> (Epictetus, *Discourses* 3.24.51, trans. Matheson 1916, vol. 2, p. 92)

When asked about our reasons for seeking virtue, Seneca says:

> 'What shall I gain,' you ask, 'if I do something good?' The gain of having done it. That is your reward; you are promised nothing else. Consider it an extra if any profit comes your way. The recompense for virtuous deeds lies in the deeds themselves.
>
> (Seneca, *On Favours* 4.1.3, trans. Timothy 1975, 35)

📖 **Read Marcus Aurelius, *Meditations* 7.73 and 9.42 (last paragraph).**

Seneca is aware that the task of 'transforming' ourselves into philosophers is a long-term objective, one that is not accomplished quickly or easily, and one that probably lasts a lifetime. Seneca begins his Letter 6, saying:

> I see in myself, Lucilius, not just an improvement but a transformation, although I would not venture as yet to assure you, or even hope, that there is nothing left in me needing to be changed. Naturally there are a lot of things about me requiring to be built up or fined down or eliminated.
>
> (Seneca, *Moral Letters* 6.1, trans. Campbell 1969, 39)

And perhaps at this early stage of our practice, we simply have to trust Seneca when he says: 'The perfection of wisdom is what makes the happy life, although even the beginnings of wisdom make life bearable' (*Moral Letters* 16.1, trans. Campbell 1969, p. 63).

📖 Read Seneca, **Letters from a Stoic, Letter 5, pp. 36–8.**

In the first part of this letter, Seneca develops the topic that we looked at in our previous paper, that of how the philosopher should live in the world which, in large part, is comprised of non-philosophers, of people who are motivated by self-interest and desires for 'indifferent' things. In Letter 7, Seneca rather cynically tells Lucilius: 'You must inevitably either hate or imitate the world.' Now, in Letter 5, Seneca tells Lucilius that, 'Inwardly everything should be different but our outward face should conform with the crowd.' At least to some degree, Seneca is advocating imitating the world.

THE CYNICS

Seneca begins by telling Lucilius that in his efforts to live the philosophical life he should adopt the right motives. It is no use trying to become a philosopher if one's real interest is to attract attention or to impress other people. 'Avoid shabby attire,' urges Seneca, 'long hair, an unkempt beard, an outspoken dislike of silverware, sleeping on the ground, and all the other misguided means to self-advertisement.' Lucilius would immediately have understood his teacher to be referring to members of the Cynic School, founded by Diogenes of Sinope four hundred years before Seneca wrote his Letters.

The Stoic School that Zeno founded about 300 BC was greatly influenced by the Cynic philosophy of his first teacher, Crates, who himself had been a student of Diogenes. The basic principles of the two schools, Stoicism and Cynicism, overlap to a great extent. Stoics and Cynics agree that virtue is the only good and is sufficient for happiness, and they agree that conventional goods are properly regarded as 'indifferents', and that the passions should be controlled and tempered.

The Cynics, however, in contrast to the Stoics, rejected all social convention as artificial and 'unnatural', and embraced an itinerant life, unencumbered by material possessions (excepting only a cloak, a staff, and a satchel for food). In this manner, the very way of life that the Cynic adopted declared unequivocally their rejection of civilised life and culture as impediments to virtue and happiness. (The term 'Cynic' – from the Greek *kunikos* – means 'dog-like', for in a variety of ways, the Cynics were seen living as dogs do, unashamed of performing natural functions in public, living without ties or possessions and feeding as beggars off the scraps that well-wishers would throw them; yet also, metaphorically, snapping at the heals of convention, trying to wake people to philosophical enlightenment by barking, so to speak, at everyone they met, and in a general sense serving as guard-dogs to defend virtue and human nature from what they see as the corrupting influences of conventional society.)

The Stoics rejected this extremism of the Cynics, believing that one can live in society in an apparently 'normal' way without being corrupted by its false values, able to make progress as a philosopher whilst also managing one's household affairs, maintaining one's relationships and engaging in the usual day-to-day activities common to philosophers (except Cynics) and non-philosophers alike.

Itinerant Cynics were common in the ancient world at this time, and no doubt Lucilius would have been aware of them, and he would have been aware of their claims that living without possessions or ties is a shortcut to virtue and happiness. Seneca warns him neither to adopt the appearance of a Cynic nor to dissociate himself from the conventions of society. As we saw in the Introduction, the Stoics saw their purpose as one of saving others from miserable lives of vice, dominated by desires for the conventional goods, and this general dedication to the service of the human race instils in those who would so serve a 'feeling of fellowship, of belonging to mankind and being members of a community', as Seneca explains. The Stoic view is that this feeling is undermined by the Cynic approach and is undermined even by adopting the *appearance* of a Cynic, if not the lifestyle itself.

> IN YOUR JOURNAL. 'Philosophy calls for simple living,' says Seneca. Read Letter 5 again, carefully picking out the examples that Seneca offers of 'simple living', and identify the benefits that follow upon adopting this way of life.

Seneca's conception of simplicity is very much that of finding a mean between complete restraint on the one hand, and extravagance on the other: 'One's life should be a compromise between the ideal and the popular morality.' In Letter 5, he mentions five areas (intended as examples, not an exhaustive list) in which we should strive for simplicity. (1) We should forgo extravagant clothes just as we should avoid slovenly dress. (2) We should not be concerned about acquiring and displaying expensive tableware. If we have gold and silver plate – admittedly this is not a good example for our own era – we should be able to regard it as no better than earthenware: and if we have only earthenware we should be able to care for it and bring it out for our guests just as if it were gold or silver. (3) We should eat a simple diet and be content with familiar dishes. (4) We should maintain basic cleanliness. (5) In the most general of senses, our homes and our furnishings should be simple. 'Anyone entering our homes should admire us rather than our furnishings.' In other words, the type of décor or furniture we have at home is essentially unimportant compared to how we conduct ourselves. It is better that people admire us for our characters rather than for our possessions.

(In the era that Seneca lived, inviting guests to dinner was a pre-eminently important aspect of social life, at least among the middle and upper classes; thus his selection of tableware and food as examples for his discussion.)

So what are the benefits of simple living? In this Letter, Seneca emphasises the Stoic philosopher's capacity to influence others, if not to follow the philosophic life, at least to moderate the excesses and shortfalls of the non-philosophic life. In short, Seneca says that we should not alienate others with overly strict practices. There is no point in setting an example that cannot be emulated.

And there are benefits that we secure for *ourselves* as seekers of happiness and peace of mind; though, there is perhaps only a weak connection between Seneca's discussion of the simple life (expanded upon in Letter 90, which we will look at later) and his discussion of the quotation from the Stoic philosopher Hecato that concludes Letter 5. Hecato is saying, in essence, that only by desiring things – things that the Stoics declare to be indifferent and which lack real value – and hoping that our desires will be fulfilled, do we open ourselves to fear and anxiety. If we set out with the hope of attaining some specific end, or some specific item of property, we immediately fall prey to anxieties that our hope will be dashed. As much as we optimistically hope for success we pessimistically fear disappointment, for no one can be sure of the final outcome of any matter, and to face life in this way is to live anxiously.

To be sure, if we live more simply we will have less to hope for, and by and large fewer outcomes will disappoint us. But as students of Stoic philosophy we strive, not to hope for outcomes that are not in our power, but to do what is sensible and appropriate with respect to the projects with which we choose to occupy ourselves, acting 'with reservation', and at all times displaying a character that embraces the virtues: which is to say, we act with self-restraint, deal with other people justly, face hardship and pain with courage, and choose our activities and carry them out wisely.

And if we do this, as we saw at the beginning of this paper, what we gain is having done it like that. We will have lived as close as our capacities permit us to what we have chosen as the best life.

THE STOIC MOTTO

Roughly halfway through Letter 5, Seneca remarks to Lucilius that: 'Our motto, as everyone knows, is to live in conformity with nature.' Seneca's sentiment in this Letter makes it clear that for Stoics, if one is to live naturally one must live simply, and that living simply is an essential component of living naturally. But what do the Stoics mean when they say – all of which mean the same thing – that we should live in agreement/in accordance/in conformity with nature? One thing that they *do not* mean is that we should 'get back to nature', go naked, or live off wild berries.

A somewhat different question from the one we have already asked and dismissed, 'If I act virtuously, what's in it for me?' is the question, 'What are the virtues *for*?' And further, we may ask what we will see is a closely related question, 'Of all the conventional goods that the Stoics refer to as preferred indifferents, which ones should I pursue, and why?' The answers to these questions will be found in seeing how the Stoics understood the nature of the world as a whole and the nature of human beings who have to cope with what happens in the world.

The Greek terms for 'nature' and 'natural' are *phusis* and *phusikos,* from where we get our modern 'physics' (the study of matter and energy) and 'physical'. The Stoics used the term *phusis* in two distinct but related ways. It is not always clear in their writings which of these two meanings are alluded to, or even, sometimes, whether *both* meanings are intended. This is the case with their motto 'Live according to nature' – which in fact is two mottoes rolled into one. One meaning is 'Live according to *human nature*' and the second meaning is 'Live according to *universal nature*'. Facts about the universe as a whole – facts about atoms and chemistry, geology and electricity, photosynthesis and enzymes – will determine the facts about the nature of individual things in the universe, including the natures of stars and planets, and of the things we find populating the surface of our world: including the nature of human beings. And clearly, human nature is distinct from the nature of other things, although some common features may be observed, as obviously there are a range of similarities between human beings and animals.

📖 **Read Marcus Aurelius,** *Meditations* **7.56.**

In a somewhat bizarre thought experiment, Marcus imagines that he has died, but that a further period of life has been granted to him. Sometimes, people who have been 'snatched from the jaws of death' – perhaps surviving an almost certainly fatal accident or medical emergency – have a strong sense that from that point the rest of their lives has been granted to them as a special gift, which they must use in some special way. I think Marcus was trying to manoeuvre himself into this perspective, from which he urges himself from that point on to live according to nature. And he means this in terms of both human nature and universal nature.

📖 **Read Marcus Aurelius,** *Meditations* **8.1.**

In this longer passage, it is clear that Marcus is discussing his own *human nature*. He tells us that 'doing what human nature requires' is found in 'having principles'. These principles we have already investigated in Paper 1, which discussed the Stoic conception of virtue (that only virtue is good and vice bad) and of the 'indifferent' things. Although Marcus does not mention it here, he would understand 'acting with reservation', which we discussed in Paper 2, also to be a 'principle' by which we 'govern every impulse and action'.

Universal nature will be covered in the next paper, but for now we will focus on the Stoic understanding of *human nature*.

All things in nature flourish after their own fashion. Different things need different circumstances and conditions in order to flourish. The specific ways in which something grows and behaves constitute its 'nature'. This being so, it is usually fairly easy to see whether anything is appropriate or inappropriate for something. It is appropriate to put the cat out for the night, but inappropriate to put the *baby* out for the night. The substances we use to 'feed' our plants are not appropriate for feeding to animals or humans. Polar bears will not survive in the tropics, and elephants will manage poorly on mountain ledges.

Like everything else in the natural world, human beings have been constituted by universal nature to have their own specific and particular nature.

> Universal Nature sanctions a norm for particular things – the nature of plants, animals and men – by reference to which they can be said to attain or not to attain their individual ends.
>
> (Long 1986, 180)

We can now see the connection between human nature and the preferred indifferents that we have already discussed. It is appropriate for humans to pursue the preferred indifferents. This is, in part at least, what is meant by 'following nature' or 'living according to nature'. We need the preferred indifferents, at least to some minimum standard, in order to flourish. We may be able to *survive* (and fall short of fully *flourishing*) by coming into possession of only a certain range of indifferent things, and by having them to an impoverished degree. Some prisoners of war held by the Japanese in the Second World War *survived*, to be sure, but they most certainly did not fully flourish.

Nature has made us capable of flourishing, and it is appropriate for us to pursue and secure what we need to flourish. Clearly we need a basic supply of food and drink, and clearly we need a basic standard of shelter. The vast majority of people flourish poorly if deprived of human contact, so clearly we need a certain quantity and quality of relationships with family and friends. Procreating and raising that family is obviously a major component for flourishing well for most people, as is having and maintaining good health. And because we live in a society, the best sort of flourishing appears to require our maintaining a certain status, to be valued and supported in the families and groups to which we belong.

Few people pursue what is inappropriate (drug addicts do, for example) and some people pursue what is appropriate in a faulty or impoverished fashion (as do criminals in their pursuit of wealth and the enjoyment of goods that rightly belong to others). Do not most people, then, 'live according to nature' just in pursuing the preferred indifferents? To make this suggestions places humans on the same level with animals, for animals pursue what is appropriate for them – that is all they can do – and doing so, for an animal, is to live according to nature.

But human beings are not animals. In important ways we are more than animals, for human beings have a faculty of reason. They can deliberate about what to do and decide whether to do it or not, whereas animals (with the possible exception of some higher primates) cannot do this. Instead, they react spontaneously and instinctively to each and every circumstance they encounter, as each arises.

Some people have a well-developed faculty of reason, whilst others do not – all the same, it remains the case that human beings are marked out as different by this faculty of reason.

> What is best in man? Reason: with this he precedes the animals and follows the Gods. Therefore perfect reason is man's peculiar good, the rest he shares with animals and plants. ... What is the peculiar characteristic of a man? Reason – which when right and perfect makes the full sum of human happiness. Therefore if every thing, when it has perfected its own good, is praiseworthy and has reached the end of its own nature, and man's own good is reason, if he has perfected reason, he is praiseworthy and has attained the end of his nature. This perfect reason is called virtue and it is identical to rectitude.
>
> (Seneca, *Moral Letters* 76.9–10, trans. Long and Sedley 1987, 63D, p. 395)

📖 Read Seneca, *Letters from a Stoic,* **Letter 41, last paragraph, pp. 88–9 (=** *Moral Letters* **41.8–9).**

In virtue of having reason, human beings can be morally good or bad, and they can adopt their interests and pursue their projects in ways entirely impossible for animals. Seneca and the Stoics see reason as the key defining difference that sets us apart from everything else in creation, and this accords reason a special status. It is indeed, supremely special. The extent to which we perfect our reason is the extent to which we approach closer to becoming fully human.

Clearly it is not enough just to pursue what is appropriate for us – for this can be done for the wrong reasons. Long (1986, 191) points out, for example, that it is appropriate to keep fit, but this does not establish that it is a good person who is keeping fit – and it certainly would not be if their motive for keeping fit is to rob a bank. Excellence of character, or virtue, is seen in a person who does what is appropriate for good reasons. This, for human beings, is what is required to live according to (*human*) nature, along with valuing virtue as good, and taking the appropriate 'external things' as 'indifferent', though preferred. What else is required to also live according to *universal* nature will be looked at in the next paper.

📖 **Read Marcus Aurelius, *Meditations* 7.11 and 5.3.**

We can now answer the question that we posed at the start of this section: 'What are virtues *for*?'

The virtues are qualities of character that make it possible for us to (1) choose from among the preferred indifferents those that are appropriate for us in (2) such a way that what we do is *right*, morally good, and praiseworthy. The faculty of reason which supports the virtues, making it possible for us to be morally good, also enables us to understand that, as we have seen, virtue is the only good, and that securing the preferred indifferents is not what matters, but the way we set about securing them; that is, by acting justly towards others, facing hardship with courage, and at all times maintaining self-restraint, and overall engaging in our affairs and choosing our path through life wisely.

In other words, our striving to be virtuous enables us to select and employ the preferred indifferents in the best possible way, without regarding them as truly good, and, if the Stoics are right, moving closer to finding a peace of mind that the ancients described as 'a smooth flow of life'.

EXERCISES

'Self-examination' is a key feature in the Stoic programme of self-development. Merely in reflecting on ourselves and our lives, as we have been doing in this course, contributes to self-examination. But as you may have noticed, writing daily Journal entries serves as an extremely effective method for focusing the mind, and helps to bring before the mind's eye ideas, connections, and insights that otherwise may well have been lost. Seneca remarks: 'A person who is not aware that he is doing anything wrong has no desire to be put right. You have to catch yourself doing it before you can reform' (Letter 28.10, trans. Campbell 1969, p. 77). We need to stand aside from ourselves, so to speak, and take an honest look at what sort of person we are, how we conduct ourselves, and how we manage our affairs and other people. We need to periodically and briefly step outside of actually living to see *how* we are doing this living, with a view to counselling ourselves – as a friend might counsel us – to make improvements; indeed, Seneca says to Lucilius, 'I am beginning to be my own friend' (Letter 6.4, trans. Campbell 1969, p. 40), and remarks that someone who can be a friend to themselves can be a friend to everyone.

> [One's mind] should be summoned each day to give account of itself. Sextius* used to do this. At the day's end, when he had retired for the night, he would interrogate his mind: 'What ailment of yours have you cured today? What failing have you resisted? Where can you show improvement? ... Could anything be finer than this habit of sifting through the whole day? Think of the sleep that follows the self-examination! How calm, deep and unimpeded it must be, when the mind has been praised or admonished and – its own sentinel and censor – has taken stock secretly of its own habits.

> I make use of this opportunity, daily pleading my case at my own court. [Seneca had been a lawyer before he turned to philosophy.] When the light has been taken away and my wife has fallen silent, aware as she is of my habit, I examine my entire day, going through what I have done and said. I conceal nothing from myself, I pass nothing by. I have nothing to fear from my errors when I can say:
>
> 'See that you do not do this any more. For the moment, I excuse you. In that dispute, you spoke too pugnaciously. Don't have anything in future to do with ignorant people – those who have never learned don't want to learn!
>
> 'You were franker than you should have been in admonishing that person. You did not help him – you just annoyed him. In future, don't just consider the truth of what you are saying, but whether the person to whom you are saying it can endure the truth. While good men are glad to be admonished, the worse a man is, the more keenly he resents any guidance.'
>
> (Seneca, *On Anger* 3.36.1–4 [with omission], trans. Cooper and Procopé 1995, 110–11)

[*Sextius is listed in the index to Campbell's *Letters from a Stoic*. He was a philosopher much admired by Seneca.]

Seneca continues this passage reminding himself to 'keep away from low company' (3.37.1), rebuking himself for losing his temper with a door-keeper and advising himself instead to 'stand back and laugh' as such obstructive and insignificant persons (3.37.2), and considers how best to deal with people who insult him or think badly of him (3.37.4–38.2).

> 📖 **Read Seneca, *Letters from a Stoic*, Letter 83, first paragraph, p. 140 (= *Moral Letters* 83.1–2).**

Here, Seneca tells Lucilius 'I shall put myself under observation straight away and undertake a review of my day.' (He proceeds to describe his day to Lucilius, though quickly veers off into a little essay about drunkenness.)

Although in carrying out our regular 'reviews of the day' we are not specifically looking for shortcomings, it is nevertheless essential that we be honest with ourselves. If, like Seneca in *On Anger* (quoted above), we do not have a very good day, we need to acknowledge that fact and, like Seneca, make resolutions to do better. Our doing this, note, is not just for the benefit of others, though indeed, others will benefit; it is for our own benefit at least as much. If we can deal fairly with others, restrain our passions, face obstacles with patience and pain with courage, and choose our path through life wisely, we will move closer to enjoying that peace and tranquillity, the desire for which moved us towards these studies in the first place.

As much as we must be honest with ourselves about our faults, we must also praise our achievements. If you cope better because you hold in mind your understanding that only virtue is good, that what matters is the way we act, not the gains or losses that result, and if you act 'with reservation', aware of your limited ability to control affairs, then all this needs to be acknowledged.

Our journals serve as a record of what we have done and the progress we have made towards the philosophic life. We may review them at any time: seeing how we coped in the past may help us to prepare for the future. The overall *point* of all this is to become more conscious, more aware, of how we are ourselves, how the world is, and how we can best live in this world.

1. So please continue writing your daily Journal in order to be your 'own friend', to counsel yourself and encourage yourself. If events are trying or even overwhelming, and you feel disappointed by your lack of progress, try to think of

what Seneca or Epictetus or Marcus Aurelius would have done or what, indeed, they would have said to you. You can pretend to talk with them, and perhaps even write down imaginary conversations.

Journals are deeply personal, so don't feel yourself under any pressure – but if you like, please send two or three examples (edited if you wish) of your Journal entries to your tutor, and please raise any questions you like either about journal-writing in general or about your specific experiences.

2. Please also continue using your Journal as a general-purpose notebook to record any thoughts or observations that you want to save, and do write down any quotations from the set books, or any other books, that you find interesting, relevant to your exercises, or inspiring in some way. Add your own comments to these quotations, so that as the months pass, you will be able to remind yourself of why these quotations struck you. (Be careful to specify the source of your quotations so that you know where they came from.)

It is also a good idea to write out in your own words definitions and descriptions of key Stoic concepts (perhaps having a special 'Glossary' section at the back of your Journal), such as 'virtue', 'external things', 'indifferents', 'what is in our power', 'acting with reservation', 'reason', and so on; and try to link what you write to the pages in these papers, and to quotations in the set books. In doing this, your Journal will develop into a very useful resource.

3. Please read Letter 90 from Seneca's *Letters from a Stoic* (pp. 161–77), which picks up on some of the themes we have looked at in this paper and also picks up on some new ones.

The picture that Seneca draws of a 'Golden Age' is almost certainly mythological, though there is every likelihood that Seneca and his fellow Romans accepted it as a fact of history. Seneca envisages the ideal life of the Golden Age to have been corrupted by greed – 'for people cease to possess everything as soon as they want everything for themselves' – whether this be greed for possessions or for power over other people.

3a. On the basis of what Seneca writes in this Letter, and on what you know generally about Stoic philosophy, explain what Seneca means when he says: 'For men in a state of freedom had thatch for their shelter, while slavery dwells beneath marble and gold' (p. 165, = *Moral Letters* 90.10). Why does Seneca use the word *slavery*? (Seneca devotes the whole of Letter 47 to the topic of slavery, and you may be interested to read this before responding to the question.)

3b. Seneca returns to a discussion of greed on page 174 (= *Moral Letters* 90.38-9). Explain why, on page 175 (= *Moral Letters* 90.41), Seneca remarks: 'We in our crimson luxury toss and turn with worry, stabbed by needling cares.'

3c. Seneca mentions greed and extravagance again (p. 164, = *Moral Letters* 90.8-9), and later he mentions luxury (p. 168, = *Moral Letters* 90.19). Please write freely on one or more of these topics. In what way have they featured in your own life? Have you ever been greedy or extravagant yourself? Have you ever pursued luxury or been envious of those who have secured it? Have you ever been taken advantage of by someone with a greedy disposition? Explain how a Stoic would set about relieving someone of their greed or extravagance or taste for luxury.

4

UNIVERSAL NATURE, GOD AND FATE

We saw in Paper 3, when discussing the Stoic motto 'Live according to nature', that the Greek term for nature, *phusis*, can be understood in two distinct senses. In the previous paper, we looked at the meaning of the motto when it is taken to indicate *human* nature, and we found that 'Live according to *human* nature', expressed as simply and most straightforwardly as possible, means: 'Live a life in which you pursue the preferred indifferents (that are appropriate to the human constitution) by undertaking your actions rationally and virtuously.'

Our considering the significance of *human* nature and its place in Stoic philosophy was done by looking inwards, so to speak, at ourselves as distinct individuals with particular needs and interests. The understanding we arrived at of the motto 'Live according to nature' can now be augmented and extended by taking 'nature' to mean *universal* nature, and by viewing the individual as a component of the wider universe.

How did the Stoics conceive of *universal* nature, the nature of the universe?

> Read Seneca, *Letters from a Stoic*, Letter 65, second paragraph, pp. 118–19 (= *Moral Letters* 65.2–4).

The topic for this paragraph is the 'two elements in the universe', and we will discuss what this means, below. The rest of the Letter – do please read it if the topic interests you – is about Plato's and Aristotle's theory of cause (as in 'cause and effect', that which brings something about) and Seneca's claim that their theories are too complicated. (He then proceeds to justify his interest in such matters, and his interest in investigating natural phenomena.)

GOD AND MATTER

The Stoics were thoroughgoing materialists, which is to say that they believed that there is just one type of thing that makes up the universe, in contrast to any number of other traditions (including, for example, the Judeo-Christian tradition and many, if not all, tribal traditions) which believe in spirits and spiritual forces which interact with the material world and which are conceived as real constituent elements of the universe. Such theories are called 'dualist', because they hold that *two* types of thing exist – matter and spirit, or matter and mind. The Stoics were therefore *monists*, because they believed that only *one* type of thing exits – matter.

The *two elements* that Seneca refers to in this extract are each understood by the Stoics to be material. One element Seneca indeed calls 'matter'. The other, referred to as 'cause', is also conceived of as matter. The first, 'matter', is thought of as passive. On its own it is just a sort of 'stuff' that is not anything in particular, that on its own cannot make anything, let alone a whole universe. The second, 'cause', is also understood to be God, God's providence (usually referred to in the ancient sources simply as 'providence'), nature, reason and fate – and this other sort of matter, which is perfectly mixed and blended with the first sort, is *active*; it is what makes things into the things they are, what gives to things their particular properties, and what brings about the endless flux of change.

> God, intelligence, fate, and Zeus are all one, and many other names are applied to him.
> (Diogenes Laertius 7.135–6, trans. Long and Sedley 1987, 46B1, p. 275)

> They [the Stoics] say that god is mixed with matter, pervading all of it and so shaping it, structuring it, and making it into the world.
> (Alexander of Aphrodisias, *On Mixture* 225,1–2, trans. Long and Sedley 1987, 45H, p. 273)

> They [the Stoics] think that there are two principles of the universe, that which acts and that which is acted upon. That which is acted upon is unqualified substance, i.e. matter; that which acts is reason [*logos*] in it, i.e. god. For this, since it is everlasting, constructs every single thing throughout all matter ...
> (Diogenes Laertius 7.134, trans. Long and Sedley 1987, 44B1–2, p. 268)

> [Balbus, the Stoic spokesman] I therefore assert that it is by the providence of the gods that the world and all its parts were first compounded and have been governed for all time.[1]
> (Cicero, *On the Nature of the Gods* 2.75, trans. Long and Sedley 1987, 54J1, p. 327)

The Stoics held God to be a sort of fiery breath that penetrates the entire cosmos and is coextensive with it. This results in God being everywhere and in everything. He turns unformed and unqualified matter into actual things (stars and planets, trees and people, etc.), and He controls what they do and how they behave. In the same way as they thought of each person having a (material) soul that was located in every part of their body and which animated and controlled that body, the Stoics thought of God as the 'soul of the universe', similarly animating and controlling the universe. This makes God immanent in the world, and not transcendent to it, for some traditions hold that God is separate and independent of the world, just as the clockmaker, who makes the clock and winds it up everyday, is transcendent to his craftsmanship.[2]

In his book, *On the Nature of the Gods*, Cicero (a Roman orator, statesman and philosopher) remarks that Cleanthes (331-232 BC, second head of the Stoic school) offered four reasons as to why people have a belief in the existence of the gods. Firstly, the skill of the soothsayers' divinatory arts was thought to be divinely inspired; secondly, the benefits and advantages that we enjoy – an adequate climate, the fertility of the soil, and so on – were put down to the operation of divine providence; thirdly, the terror instilled in people by natural phenomena such as lightning, storms, plagues, earthquakes, comets and other things led them to suspect that a divine power must be at work in bringing them about; and fourthly, the most compelling reason for the existence of the gods, was the order, regularity and beauty observed in astronomical phenomena. Cicero continues this account by remarking that:

> Just as, if someone enters a house, a gymnasium or a forum, when he sees the controlled methodical pattern of all that goes on he cannot think that these things happen without cause, but understands that there is someone in charge who is obeyed, much more must he, in the case of these great motions and phases and of the orderings of things so numerous and immense, none of which has ever been reported otherwise by a tradition of measureless

antiquity, conclude that it is by some mind that these great motions of nature are controlled.

> (Cicero, *On the Nature of the Gods* 2.15, trans. Long and Sedley 1987, 54C6, p. 324)

What this account is suggesting is that at least some people believe that there must be a *reason* as to why things are as they are and why things happen as they do. God, as the second sort of matter that blends with and shapes the first sort of 'passive' matter into physical objects whose destiny He shapes, is the ultimate *explanation for everything*.

📖 **Read Seneca, *Letters from a Stoic*, Letter 41, focusing on page 87 (= *Moral Letters* 41.3–5).**

Whereas Cleanthes points to such things as thunder and lightning, storms and earthquakes as indicating a divine presence in the world, in complete contrast Seneca recounts his tranquil experience of a 'dense wood of ancient trees'. Merely in pausing to open ourselves to the majesty and beauty of such a place we can be 'persuaded of the presence of a deity'. The Stoics believed that the universe is governed by forces that are intelligent and reasoning, as well as self-aware – and these forces are the gods, or God, for it all comes to the same thing. Just as we are rational animals in virtue of the sort of souls that we have, God, as the soul of the universe, is said by the Stoics to be a rational (and immortal) animal.

> What is god? The mind of the universe. What is god? All that you see and all that you do not see.
>
> (Seneca, *Natural Questions* Pref. 13)

Some people can occasionally have a 'religious experience', similar to Seneca's experience in the woods or the cave, in which they have a strong sense that there is some ineffable power that orders events and structures the world. In such a state of mind, one can spontaneously have a strong sense that everything makes sense, that all is well, and perhaps have an insight into one's role in life. After such an experience one may return to daily life with renewed energy and confidence, or make some important change that has long been due.

> ✎ **IN YOUR JOURNAL. If you can recall ever having had an experience of this sort, or anything like it, please write an account of it in your Journal. How well does it agree with the Stoic understanding of the nature of the universe? What significance did it have for you?**

Alas, not everyone has had this type of experience, and possibly it is very rare. Those among us who have not enjoyed any such insight should not be discouraged, and should live in hope that some sort of meaningful revelation can come at any moment.

CAUSE AND FATE

The Stoics believed that everything that happens is *fated* to happen, and that all that happens is for the best. The notion of 'fate' is explained and defined in terms of 'cause'.

> They [the Stoics] say that this world is a unity which includes all existing things in itself and is governed by a living, rational, intelligent nature. This government of existing things in the world is an everlasting one that proceeds in a linked and ordered sequence. The things that happen first are causes for those that happen after them. In this way

they are all bound together with each other; neither does anything happen in the world such that something else does not unconditionally follow upon it and is attached to it as cause, nor again can any of the following events be detached from the preceding events so as not to follow from one of them as if bound together with it. Every event has its consequent which is by necessity linked to it as cause, and every event has something before it to which it is linked as cause. Nothing in the world exists or comes to be without a cause, because nothing in the world is detached and separated from all the things that preceded it. For the cosmos would be torn apart and divided, and would no longer remain a unity for ever, governed by a single ordering and economy, if a causeless motion were introduced; and that would be introduced if it were not the case that all existing things and events have antecedent causes, upon which they follow of necessity [...] The very fate, the nature, and the reason, in accordance with which the whole is governed – this they say is God, and it is in all things that exist and come to pass, and it thus makes use of the proper nature of all the things that exist for the economy of the whole.
(Alexander of Aphrodisias, *On Fate* 191.30–192.28, trans. David Furley, in Algra et. al 1999, 450)

The theory that everything is caused is referred to by philosophers as the theory of *causal determinism*, and is often discussed in conjunction with the theory of free will, in that if everything is caused to happen just as it does by prior events, must it not be the case that someone's mental acts (of believing or judging or intending) are also caused by prior events? And if they are, human beings appear not to be able to do anything of their own volition, for everything that we suppose them to do freely – even their *thinking* that they are acting freely – is caused by prior events.

The 'determinism versus free will' debate has been a lively and contentious issue in philosophy from ancient times to the present day, and although the problem may now be better understood, it has nevertheless not yet been adequately resolved.

For our present purposes we need not get embroiled in this debate. Our excuse for this rests on these two points. (1) Each of us is fully convinced that we are the authors of our own actions, and that we are responsible (and sometimes culpable) for what we do. (2) It would be quite impossible to live as we do if we did not believe this. And we may say further that (3) our own actions are nevertheless *not* at all divorced from the causal nexus that constitutes the history of the world, for we always have reasons to act as we do (even if those reasons are not always good ones), and those reasons only make sense when they refer to events happening in the world, and our actions contribute to how the world becomes; that is, we cause things to happen, and this is why, at least in part, the causal history of the world is how it is.

To sum up: The entire sequence of causes which stretches out to form the entire history of the world, as described by Alexander in the previous extract, was called by the ancients, fate.

> The Stoics [describe fate as] a sequence of causes, that is, an inescapable ordering and interconnexion.
> (Aetius I.28.4, trans. Long and Sedley 1987, 55J, p. 336)

> In On Providence book 4, Chrysippus says that fate is a certain natural everlasting ordering of the whole: one set of things follows on and succeeds another, and the interconnexion is inviolable.
> (Aulus Gellius 7.2.3, trans. Long and Sedley 1987, 55K, p. 336)

'LIVE ACCORDING TO UNIVERSAL NATURE'

We already know what the Stoics meant when they issued their injunction to live according to human nature. Once we recognise the facts about human nature, and once we accept the Stoic understanding of what is truly good and bad, we should live in such a way that we pursue the preferred indifferents virtuously.

Now that we have been introduced to the Stoic notions of God and matter, cause and fate, we will be able to see what we should do in order to live according to universal nature.

> 📖 Read Marcus Aurelius, *Meditations* 4.40, 6.1, 6.38, 7.9, 10.5 and 10.20.

Marcus picks out five key themes in these extracts:

(1) The universe is a single living being comprised of one god pervading one substance (4.40, 7.9), and all things are created and directed by its will (6.1).

(2) Everything works in conjunction with everything else, one thing following upon another, so as to 'cause all that comes to be' (4.40, 6.38).

(3) This 'interweaving' and 'mutual intertwining' of causes and effects creates a 'densely woven fabric' in which all things are 'bound up together and interrelated' (4.40, 6.38, 7.9).

(4) This process is intelligent (i.e., 'reason governs it') and the reason that pervades the densely woven fabric of the universe is 'common to all intelligent creatures' (6.1, 7.9).

(5) This intelligence has no capacity for 'bringing about anything bad' for it cannot do anything wrong and nothing can be injured by it (6.1), in that everything is

made to contribute to the benefit of everything else in exactly the right way (6.38, 7.9, 10.20).

Thus, for the Stoics, God, fate, the universe and its history are in reality the same thing. Which is why from our own subjective perspectives, we may consider that everything that befalls us in life has been 'pre-ordained'; that from the beginning of creation the web of fate has been woven (intelligently) to result (at this moment in the history of the world) in our being exactly who we are, facing whatever it is we face, our realising this to be the case, or not (10.5).

📖 **Read Marcus Aurelius, *Meditations* 5.27.**

When Marcus says that God and human beings (and other sentient, self-conscious creatures, should there be any) share one common intelligence, he means in fact that our own minds are literally fragments of God. So, in aiming to live according to nature, over and above our embracing intellectually the account we have explored in this section of the paper, we should realise that in striving to perfect our own natures, we are in fact contributing to the perfection of the whole world. At least to some tiny extent, it is through our own actions that God brings about the world as it should be.

Plato, whose work along with other philosophical outlooks inspired the early Stoics, said this:

> Let us persuade the young men by arguments that all things have been arranged by the overseer of the universe for the security and excellence of the whole; and the parts of the universe each act or are acted upon appropriately according to their capacity. Each of these parts down to the smallest feature of its condition or activity is under the direction of ruling powers, which have perfected every minutest detail. And you, you stubborn man, are one of

these parts, minute though you are, which always contributes to the good of the whole. You have failed to see that every act of creation occurs for the sake of the universe, that it may enjoy a life of well-being; creation occurs not for your sake but you occur for the sake of the universe. ... You are peeved because you fail to realize how what is best for you is best for the universe as well as yourself.

(Plato, *Laws* 903b–d, trans. Long 1986, 151)

📖 **Read Marcus Aurelius, *Meditations* 5.8.**

Marcus offers us an analogy: what fate brings to us we should accept in the same way that we accept a prescription for treating an illness. In the same way that some specific treatment may not be especially agreeable, so too may we find that what fate 'prescribes' is not altogether to our liking. As we have already seen, and as Marcus repeats in this extract, we should 'welcome whatever comes to us' because it contributes to the 'health of the universe'.

📖 **Read Marcus Aurelius, *Meditations* 7.57 and 12.32.**

In these extracts Marcus goes beyond saying that we should (merely) accept our fate, for now he says that we should '*love* what universal nature brings'.

For those among us who have had the good fortune to enjoy a religious experience that to be sure a few individuals do indeed report, such that they have had a direct perception or deep intuitive understanding that all the things we have said in this paper are essentially true – for such people, maybe we can understand that no matter how disappointing or frustrating or sheer unpleasant one's fate appears to be, nevertheless, that fate can be welcomed and 'loved'.

But almost certainly, we will not fall into that (probably small) number. Many of us will be able to appreciate these teachings on an intellectual level, and be able to declare with strong conviction that there is a God who created and sustains the world, and that we stand to such a being, and to the world at large, much as the Stoics claim. But that won't of itself relieve us of the burden of living, of finding, alas, too many things a source of distress, and dwelling on how unfit and unready we are to deal with serious problems, including illness and death (both our own, and others').

It is not clear whether Marcus was truly able to embrace the metaphysical stance that he writes about, or whether he wrote what he did to encourage himself towards a goal he never achieved. It may well be the case that in fact no one has achieved this goal, that there never has been anyone who has been able to say honestly that right at the core of their being is the strongest imaginable conviction that God has ordered everything for the best, that human suffering is really just an illusion which we create for ourselves by making the mistake of simply not regarding things properly.

The Stoic decides to persist in trying to 'make progress'. They remind themselves that they are blessed with a faculty of reason which they can use to appreciate what has true value and what is truly good. A Stoic can be regarded, perhaps, as someone who continually reminds themselves that their plight is not as bad as it may appear, and that our capacities, to deal with both the petty frustrations of daily life and significant turns of bad fortune, are superior (with philosophy's aid) to how we usually imagine them.

We see these ideas expressed clearly in Seneca's essay, *On Providence*, from which the following three extracts are taken:

> What is the duty of the good man? To offer himself to Fate. [...] His path will not be level, he but must go uphill and down, he must be wave-tossed and steer his craft

through troubled waters, he must maintain his course in the face of Fortune. Much that is hard and rough will befall him, but he will himself soften it and smooth it down.

(Seneca, *On Providence* 5.8–9 [with omission], trans. Hadas 1958, 42)

'Yet why does god allow evil to happen to good men?' But in fact he does not. From good men he keeps every evil away – sin and crime and wicked thoughts and greedy schemes and blind lust and avarice which covets another's property. The good man himself, god protects and defends; should anyone expect that god will look after the good man's baggage also? Good men release god from this care, for they themselves despise externals. Democritus cast his riches away in the belief that they were a burden to a good mind. Then why should you wonder that god allows a good man to light upon a lot which a good man would sometimes himself choose to light upon? Good men lose their sons: why not, when they sometimes leave their country of their own accord never to return? They are slain: why not, when they sometimes lay hands upon themselves? Why do they suffer certain hardships? To teach others to endure them; they were born to serve as models.

Imagine that god speaks as follows: 'What grounds do you have to complain of me, you who have opted for righteousness? Other men I have surrounded with spurious goods, I have beguiled their empty minds, as it were, with a long and deceptive dream. I have adorned them with gold and silver and ivory, but there is nothing good inside. The men you look upon as happy, if you could see not their outward appearance but their inward nature, are wretched, squalid, mean.

(Seneca, *On Providence* 6.1–4, trans. Hadas 1958, 43–4)

But to you I have given goods that are sure and abiding, goods which are better and greater the more one turns them about and scrutinizes them from every side. To you I have granted scorn of terrors and disdain of passions. You do not shine outwardly because all your goods are turned inward. [...] Your whole good I have bestowed within yourselves: your good fortune is not to need good fortune.

'"But," you object, "many things which are sad and dreadful and hard to bear do happen." Because I could not make you evade their assault, I have given your minds armor to withstand them; bear them with fortitude. In this respect you can surpass god: he is exempt from enduring evil, you rise superior to it. Scorn poverty: no one is as poor as he was at birth. Scorn pain: either it will go away or you will. Scorn death: either it finishes you or it transforms you. Scorn Fortune: I have given her no weapon with which to strike your soul.'

(Seneca, *On Providence* 6.5–6 [with omission], trans. Hadas 1958, 44)

EXERCISES

Please continue writing your daily Journal as a means of focusing your thoughts and becoming more conscious of how you experience things and respond to events. Remind yourself as often as you need to that, as the Stoics see it, excellence for a human being consists in living virtuously, and that living in this way means valuing things in terms of how they benefit our projects, and that only acting well (= acting virtuously) is truly good. Remind yourself constantly to 'act with reservation'.

If it seems appropriate, please review the course papers and your own Journal notes and entries. Review also your 'Glossary of Terms' if you have started one (see Paper 3, Exercise 2); you may find that you can add to your entries, finding new formulations or new quotations from the ancient writers that help you to consolidate your understanding.

Remind yourself that 'living simply' is the ideal for the wise person, and be alert to making changes or even turning down opportunities if doing so will contribute to this ideal. Record your decisions and actions accurately and fully in your Journal. If some decision is challenging, record that this is so, for the *thinking* that writing requires may well serve to clarify the issue in question.

1. Explain what the Stoics mean by the following terms:
   (a) Matter
   (b) God
   (c) Fate

2. Please read Letter 107 from Seneca's *Letters from a Stoic* (pp. 197–200), which discusses some of the topics we have looked at in this paper. Lucilius' slaves have run away, and we are to imagine that he has written to Seneca and revealed how upset he is by this event. In general terms Seneca says that Lucilius is being a bit silly to worry so much about this setback.

   Imagine that you are Lucilius making a reply to Seneca's Letter in order to clarify what he is advising you. Please put yourself in Lucilius' position and continue your letter from this opening sentence: 'Thank you for your advice about how I should deal with the loss of my slaves ... '

3. How does the Stoic 'see to it that nothing takes them by surprise'?

4. Towards the end of Letter 107, Seneca introduces military service as a metaphor for life. Explain how this metaphor works.

5. Seneca attempts to make a case for hardships and misfortunes being *beneficial* to the wise person:

> Among the many magnificent sayings of our friend Demetrius is the following [...] it still rings and reverberates in my ears. 'No one is more unhappy, in my judgment,' says he, 'than a man who has never met with adversity.' He has never had the privilege of testing himself. Everything has come easily to him according to his wish; yet the gods' judgment of him has been unfavorable. He was deemed unworthy of ever vanquishing Fortune, which shuns any cowardly antagonist, as if to say, 'Why should I take on that kind of opponent? He will lay his arms down at once, and I will not need to use my full strength against him. A threatening gesture will rout him; he cannot face my grim expression. I must look around for someone else with whom to match my strength; I am ashamed to fight a man who is ready to be beaten.'
>
> (Seneca, *On Providence* 3.3, trans. Hadas 1958, 33)

> To triumph over the disasters and terrors of mortal life is the privilege of the great man. [...] You are a great man, but how can I know, if Fortune has never given you a chance to display your prowess? [...] 'I account you unfortunate because you have never been unfortunate. You have passed through life without an adversary; no man can know your potentiality, not even you.' For self-knowledge, testing is necessary; no one can discover what he can do except by trying. [...] Do not, I beseech you, dread the things which the immortal gods apply to our souls like goads; disaster is virtue's opportunity. [...] Cruelty presses hardest on the inexperienced [...] So god hardens and scrutinizes and exercises those he approves and loves;

but those he appears to indulge and spare he is only keeping tender for disasters to come.

(Seneca, *On Providence* 4.1–7 [with omissions], trans. Hadas 1958, 36–8)

How do you respond to this analysis? Would you choose a life of absolute ease, entirely devoid of any hardship or disappointment, were such a choice to be yours? Is life a test, as Seneca suggests?

6. For some people, their religious beliefs are deeply personal and wholly private. Depending upon your own feelings about this, please feel free not to send in a response to this question (though you may wish to record some private notes).

Has your investigations of the Stoic notion of God made any difference to your own beliefs?

NOTES

1. 'God' and 'gods' for the Stoics identify the same thing – that which brings about the universe and makes things the way they are. '[God] is the creator of the whole and, as it were, the father of all, both generally and, in particular, that part of him which pervades all things, which is called by many descriptions according to his powers. For they call him Zeus [*Dia*] as the cause [*di' hon*] of all things; Zên in so far as he is responsible for, or pervades, life [*zên*]; Athena because his commanding-faculty stretches into the aether; Hera because it stretches into the air; ... [etc.]' (Diogenes Laertius 7.147, trans. Long and Sedley 1987, 54A, p. 323).
2. The terms 'world', 'universe' and 'cosmos' in this discussion (and commonly in contemporary philosophical discourse) mean the same thing, that is, 'all there is'.

5

LIVING IN SOCIETY

Everything we do is done with respect to other people and with regard to our living in human society. We live in a rich and complex community in which, in deeply complicated ways, everyone is dependent upon everyone else. To take a simple example, it is immediately obvious that the young infant is entirely dependent upon his or her mother. But in order to carry on the business of parenthood, to feed, to clothe, and to provide medicines for her child, the mother is of course dependent upon a whole network of other people. Should there ever have been an individual who lived in a completely self-sufficient manner, entirely independently of others, we must say that such a person is an exceptionally rare and unusual phenomenon. Some few people do nevertheless maintain that they are self-sufficient, relying on no one, uncomfortable with the very idea that they are supported by others and that they in turn have obligations to contribute to the society in which they live. Indeed, some people like this have been known to declare that there is no such thing as society, and to prefer a view of the world in which each individual acts selfishly in pursuit of their own interests, essentially unmoved by the plight of others who have needs that they are powerless to fulfil for themselves. At best, such a view is ignorant and mistaken: at worst it reveals of those holding it a lack of humanity.

If the network of support and co-operation that binds people into communities were to weaken beyond a certain point or fail altogether, it is readily apparent that human culture would end.

> Stoic arguments seek the health of the individual human being, to be sure. But as they do so, they never let the pupil forget that pursuing this end is inseparable from seeking the good of other human beings. For philosophy's mission ... is not to one person or two, not to the rich or the well-educated or the prominent, but to the human race as such. And all human beings, following philosophy, should understand themselves to be linked to all other human beings, in such a way that the ends of individuals are intertwined, and one cannot pursue one's fullest good without at the same time caring for and fostering the good of others.
> (Nussbaum 1994, 341–2)

In discussing how we should live in society and how Stoicism approaches this question, Seneca says:

> No school has more goodness and gentleness; none has more love for human beings, nor more attention to the common good. The goal which it assigns to us is to be useful, to help others, and to take care, not only of ourselves, but of everyone in general and of each one in particular.
> (Seneca, *On Clemency* 3.3, trans. Hadot 1998, 231)

In this paper we shall look at how the Stoic lives in society, and how they deal with the realities of daily interaction with others.

📖　**Read Marcus Aurelius, *Meditations* 2.1.**

In this entry of his notebook, Marcus undeniably paints a gloomy prospect of the coming day. No doubt he will also meet with competent, honest and faithful people, if not frequently, then at least some of the time. But Marcus' present task is to remind himself how he should respond to the 'meddling, ungrateful, violent, treacherous, envious, and ungrateful' people with whom he anticipates coming into contact. Many people either rarely or never take the trouble to consciously think through how best to deal with 'difficult people'. Perhaps because such difficult people just are a fact of life, many people, most of the time, simply respond to them on a moment by moment basis, getting angry (not necessarily in their presence), being critical, or even plotting against them, as seems appropriate on some intuitive level. Operating in such an ad hoc fashion is, fairly clearly, unlikely to encourage any real improvements on the part of difficult people, and it certainly does not promote a tranquil and unperturbed life for those who employ this approach.

The Stoics claim that it is entirely possible to live amongst, and to work with, difficult people at the same time as remaining wholly unruffled and undisturbed by their actions. It may even be possible, with judicious care, to reform such people. Indeed, as has been indicated previously, the Stoics were famous for their unfailing serenity.

> **IN YOUR JOURNAL. In paragraph 2.1 Marcus makes several different points that, if he can bear them in mind and act appropriately in consequence, will enable him to retain his Stoic serenity in the midst of any upset caused by difficult people. Carefully read this paragraph again, and identify the points that Marcus makes.**

(1) For the Stoics, the fact that people behave badly has a strikingly obvious explanation: **they have 'no knowledge of good and bad'**. Difficult people simply do not see things the way the Stoic does. Rather, they value indifferent things and feel threatened when the indifferent things in which they are interested are themselves threatened. But Marcus, having 'beheld the nature of the good' knows that he himself cannot be harmed by anything that difficult people do. The harm they cause is in fact self-inflicted, and results from their having not been shown that the good for human beings consists in developing and exercising a virtuous (i.e., excellent) character. (2) Nevertheless, even difficult people possess a rationality which is identical to that of the Stoic sage – it's just that for these people their rationality has not been tutored. Marcus reminds himself that **difficult people have a nature that is 'akin' to his own, in that all people share with him a mind that is a portion of the divine mind of God**. (3) In consequence of this insight Marcus declares that **he cannot be harmed by such people** (as we noted above), and further (4) **he has no grounds to be angry with them** (5) **nor to hate them**.

(6) The idea of sharing a common nature (the rationality and mind of God) is extended to embrace the idea that **all people 'come into being to work together'** – upon which Marcus gives us the examples of a foot, a hand, an eyelid or one row of teeth, none of which can function properly without their opposite number. (7) Indeed, **'to work against one another is contrary to nature'**, is contrary to how we have been created and what is proper to us as sentient, self-conscious creatures. Specifically, to be angry with someone is to 'work against them', and is contrary to nature, which means it is contrary to *our* natures as human beings endowed with reason.

These points merit further investigation.

THE STOIC ACCOUNT OF WHY PEOPLE ACT AS THEY DO

📖 Read Marcus Aurelius, *Meditations* 6.27, 7.26, 8.14 and 10.37.

People pursue what they believe will benefit them. Their capacity to judge what is truly beneficial may be, as the Stoics think, flawed, but all the same says Marcus, they have the right to 'strive after what they regard as suitable and beneficial' (6.27). Our becoming upset at the actions of others, Marcus suggests, denies them the right to do as they see fit. This idea is expanded upon in 7.26 where Marcus talks in terms of a 'conception of good and evil'. Clearly, those aiming to perfect their characters as Stoics hold a very different view of what is truly good and bad (as we saw in Paper 1), and it is perfectly obvious why bad people do bad things; from their own perspective what they do is *good*, since they benefit from what they do, or at least they think they do. Seeing that this is the case, not only can we understand why people do bad things, we begin to anticipate what they are likely to actually do. If we attempt to answer Marcus' question, 'What ideas does this person hold on human goods and ills?' (8.14) we may even be able to second-guess someone's actions. If we do this well, what they do 'will not seem extraordinary or strange', indeed, what they do can be regarded as inevitable, given their beliefs, to the extent that those beliefs 'constrain' the agent to act as they do.

But in trying to understand other people, we must not loose sight of trying to understand *ourselves*. In 10.37 Marcus reminds us to examine ourselves before we examine others. With respect to our own actions it is imperative that we ask of ourselves, 'What is *my* aim in performing this action?' To be sure, finding ways of responding to this question has been the underlying project of the present course.

ACCEPTING OTHER PEOPLE

📖 Read Marcus Aurelius, *Meditations* 5.17, 5.25, 7.1 and 7.22.

Other people do what they do because they think it is for the best. And we have to accept that, and decide to remain calm and untroubled when we find ourselves affected by the actions of 'people of bad character' (5.17). If someone harms us, that is *their* affair (5.25). Our responsibility as Stoics who claim to possess the insights of philosophical wisdom is to respond with virtuous actions on every occasion.

We may mistake Marcus' tone in 7.1 for pessimism. Certainly he is resigned, but that resignation results from powerful and deeply cherished philosophical principles. As we saw in the previous paper, Stoics believe that we have been assigned our own unique destiny which we have a duty to live up to. Bad behaviour, 'vice', just is a fact of life for human beings – it is a part of everyone's destiny. Do not be surprised when it is encountered, for 'This is something that you have often seen.'

One of the readings for Paper 4 was Chapter 7.57 from the *Meditations*, where Marcus says: 'Love only that which falls to you and is spun as the thread of your destiny; for what could be better suited to you?' Specifically, in 7.22, Marcus says that we should love 'those who stumble', and that such love will arise in us when we recall that such people 'do wrong through ignorance and against their will'. Marcus concludes by remarking that in any event, the 'wrongdoer' cannot actually harm us, because the only harm we can suffer is to fall into vice, as we saw in Paper 1; only our *projects* can suffer harm, whereas we ourselves as moral agents are invulnerable. Should we think we are harmed – subject to our not falling into vice – we would be mistaken.

THE EQUANIMITY OF THE WISE PERSON

Sometimes we fall prey to foolish or malicious people, who think badly of us and who attempt to portray us in a bad light for reasons, we now recognise, that make sense from *their* perspective.

> 📖 **Read Marcus Aurelius, *Meditations* 4.18, 9.27 and 9.34.**

The Stoic remains completely indifferent to what other people think or say of them. As practitioners of the Stoic art of living, it makes no difference to us and our capacity for acting well that other people may be thinking badly of us or spreading malicious gossip. We must remind ourselves often that when the bad person supposes that 'their criticisms harm or their praises bring benefit' (9.34), they are simply mistaken. And we must not make the same mistake ourselves by believing that their criticisms or praises mean anything to us.

If we are confident that we are acting as we should, there is no need for us to think even for a moment of amending our actions in the hope that others who have criticised us will come to approve of us. Not that criticism should always be dismissed out of hand, for we should remain alert to the possibility that we have made a mistake and need to do something differently. But when we do adjust our course, this is done not to appease criticisms (though such appeasement may in fact occur), but in order that we should do the right thing.

And just as the gods show goodwill to bad people 'through dreams and oracles' by means of which they obtain the indifferent things that they want, we should likewise show goodwill (9.27).

📖 Read Marcus Aurelius, *Meditations* 5.32, 10.30 and 11.13.

In a way, it would be rather silly for one living the philosophical life to be troubled by an 'ignorant and uncultivated soul' (5.32). And it would be wholly unacceptable to get angry with such people, or for us not to 'soon forget our anger' (10.30) once it has arisen. For feeling anger towards wrongdoers would amount to discarding, or at least temporarily forgetting, the bulk of Stoic teaching. To accept this teaching, in part, is to accept that we do not in fact have anything to feel angry about.

Marcus points to the core of Stoic ethics in 11.13 where he reminds himself that the person who feels contempt or hatred for him must look to their own thoughts and actions. *For this is in that person's power.* How Marcus will react to this person is in *his* power, and this is where he will apply himself, to make sure that he never does anything that merits contempt or hatred. And this is done by striving on all occasions to do what is appropriate, demonstrating virtuous thought and action, and aiming to make progress in the development of an excellent character. Although we seek no reward in adopting this way of life, if we find ourselves 'neither disposed to be angry at anything nor make any complaint' (11.13) we will be in receipt of the serenity for which the most outstanding Stoics were famed.

WORKING WITH OTHERS

Marcus points out in 11.13 that we should be 'kind and good-natured to everyone, and ready to show this particular person the nature of his error'. So the Stoic philosopher, although indifferent to the behaviour of others, does not remain wholly aloof and wholly disinterested in their conduct.

As we will now see, Stoics believe that they have a responsibility to promote a well-ordered and harmonious society.

📖 Read Marcus Aurelius, *Meditations* 4.4, 9.23 and 12.26.

The responsibility that the Stoics believe they have to always treat people fairly and considerately, not to get angry with them nor to chastise them without at least making the attempt to teach them better ways, stems from the fact that we are all 'fellow-citizens' (4.4). The state of which we are 'fellow-citizens' is not, on the Stoic view, the state in which we happen to reside or to which we owe some patriotic duty, but is the state comprising the entirety of rational beings. Recognising this to be the case, the Stoic realises that their responsibility to perfect their own character must extend to serving the community of rational beings as a whole by embracing the duty to 'contribute to the perfecting of social life' (9.23). Precisely because other people are also rational, or at least have the potential for rationality, the Stoic thereby becomes responsible for others no less than he or she is responsible for themselves. The Stoic injunction to adopt and live by the virtues makes sense only if there is some readily identifiable medium in which virtuous activity can take place, and clearly that medium is the society in which we live, conceived (in today's terms) as the global human community. Furthermore, to briefly broach a topic that has been omitted from this course, many present-day Stoics will be in agreement that our responsibilities extend beyond the human community to the global environment as a whole, with respect to which we have deep obligations of responsible stewardship, as more and more people (most of them non-Stoic, of course) are coming to realise.

The Stoic aims at the betterment of the individual and the betterment of society both at the same time. If someone behaves better than they did before, this is of course better for that individual, but it is also better for society at large.

This is why, not only does the Stoic not get angered by the bad behaviour of others, but will also 'instruct them ... and show them the truth' (6.27).

> 📖 **Read Marcus Aurelius, *Meditations* 8.59, 9.11 and 12.16.**

Again (as we saw in 9.27) Marcus suggests that we should model our response to bad people on the gods, pointing out that the gods are kind to such people, helping them 'to certain ends, to health, to wealth, to reputation' (9.11; see also 7.70), and that our own capacity to be kind has been granted *to us* by the gods expressly for this purpose. In this Chapter (9.11), Marcus gives the impression that being kind is a fall-back position we should adopt if our primary purpose to show people 'the error of their ways' should fail. It is fairly clear, though, that Marcus understands trying to help others to be the supreme act of kindness, for we have seen that he talks in terms of having love for those who 'do wrong through ignorance' (7.22; see also: 6.39, 7.13, 7.31, 7.65 and 11.1).

> 📖 **Read Marcus Aurelius, *Meditations* 8.23, 8.43, 11.4 and 11.18.**

These extracts from the *Meditations* serve as a summary of the points we have discussed in this paper. The 'Ninth Rule' in 11.18 provides us with basic guidelines as to how we should 'show them the error of their ways' (9.11). There is a real danger that, in trying to 'persuade them' (6.50), the Stoic philosopher will come across as a pompous, self-righteous, interfering busybody. Indeed, in 10.36, Marcus imagines that in his final moments as he lies dying, there will be some around him who will be pleased to see the back of him, ready to say: 'What a relief to be finally freed from this schoolmaster; not that he was ever harsh with any of us, but I could sense that he was silently condemning us.' (*Meditations* 10.36, trans. Hard.) We cannot contribute to the betterment of society and to the improvement of the individual if everything we say is rejected as self-opinionated imposition.

Yet we have been blessed with a philosophical insight granted to only a few people, and this being so imposes a duty on us, if not to urge everyone to become a Stoic, then at least to encourage people to pay closer attention to what should really matter to them as human beings and to the effects their actions have upon the welfare of others and upon their own interests.

> **IN YOUR JOURNAL.** Read the 'Ninth Rule' of *Meditations* **11.18** again, and specify precisely the attitudes that Marcus says we should adopt when advising others of their errors.

When dealing with other people we must consistently be kind and sincere, and our actions and words must not be 'hypocritical or a mere façade' (as they would be, for instance, were we trying to encourage someone to moderate or eliminate their anger, whilst being known for having an uncontrollable temper ourselves). We should advise people 'quietly' and 'mildly', even whilst they are attempting to harm us. We must be tactful and advise without being sarcastic or reproachful, ignoring any temptations to 'impress the bystanders'; and if we are aware that bystanders are present, we should simply disregard them and proceed to offer advice 'as one person to another'.

Nobody likes to be reproached, and advice that aims to be friendly, considerate and kind can all the same often come across as negative criticism, mistaken as intending to shame and degrade. Nobody likes to be condemned, and trying to mend people's ways will often be met with a hurtful and affronted rejection.

> On a warm and sultry day, when Epictetus was sitting quietly at home, a neighbor came to seek his advice. After the usual friendly greetings, the neighbor said:
> 'When my father died my elder brother took possession of our farm, and he makes me work for him from morning till night, giving me only sufficient food and clothing for a bare existence. How can I compel him to give me a fair share of my father's estate?'
> EPICTETUS: Philosophy promises no one any material benefit; otherwise it would be promising something beyond its power. The material a philosopher works with is the art of living contentedly.
> NEIGHBOR: Well, what about my brother's ill behavior?
> EPICTETUS: That is a matter for your brother's concern; not yours.
> NEIGHBOR: How then, is his ill treatment of me to be corrected?
> EPICTETUS: Bring him to me and I will speak to him, but I have nothing to say to you, nor do I make any promise to you about his behavior.
> NEIGHBOR: But supposing after you speak to him, he still refuses to treat me fairly? Isn't there any way whereby he can be compelled to do so?
> EPICTETUS: Nothing worthwhile is created suddenly any more than a grape or a fig is created overnight. If you tell me that you want a fig, I will answer that the growth and development of a fig takes time. First, the fig tree must grow and blossom; later the tree will bear fruit, which later still must mature and ripen. As a fig tree

> does not bear fruit suddenly, don't expect the fruit of
> the human mind to be created instantaneously.
> (Epictetus, *Discourses* 1.15, paraphrase
> by Bonforte 1974, 72)

There are no guarantees when it comes to trying to mend someone's bad behaviour, and, in any event, the Stoic philosopher will pursue such a course 'with reservation'. Epictetus will speak to the bad brother, but he cannot promise that his words will make any difference. Mending the bad brother's unkind and unjust attitudes is something that Epictetus and his neighbour must cultivate, as one would cultivate a fig tree. One must be subtle and one must be patient.

If the bad ways of human beings could be cured quickly and easily with no more than a whisper of good advice, then we would be living in a world very different from the one we in fact inhabit, for in that world the quantity of human evil would be minuscule, and hardly more than a glance of disapproval would be required to correct the most diabolical of schemes. But as Epictetus intimates, turning people from bad ways is a most uncertain business. But it is right that we should attempt it. When we fail, or when we secure only limited results, we will have to accept that we have done the right thing, and we must nevertheless go on living in a world in which bad people go about their business, just as they did all those centuries ago when Epictetus tried to advise his neighbour.

> One day when Epictetus entered the Agora, he heard his students arguing heatedly about the punishment that should be inflicted upon a thief and an adulterer. After listening to the heated discussion for several minutes, Epictetus said to the obvious spokesman of the group, 'Why are you so angry at these men? Shouldn't you pity

them because they are ignorant of what is for their good and what is for their evil? Show them the error of their ways and you will see that they will correct their faults. If they do, you will have the pleasure of knowing that you have helped convert evil men to good men, but if they don't mend their ways, they will continue to be what they are, men of evil.'

SCHOLAR: Shouldn't these men be destroyed before they commit more crimes in our village?

EPICTETUS: No. These men are blind; not in their vision that distinguishes white from black, but in their Reason, that distinguishes good from evil. If your question is stated on the basis of reason, it would be similar to your saying, 'Shouldn't this blind man and that deaf man be destroyed, because one is blind and the other is deaf?'

SCHOLAR: But, if we set these men free, what guarantee do we have that they will not repeat their crime and thus set an example for others to do the same?

EPICTETUS: Let me state once again the basic rule of our philosophy: the greatest harm that a person can suffer is the loss of the most valuable possession, his Reason. The harm he creates for himself is not transferred to others. Therefore, there is no reason for others to become angry because a person commits a crime against himself.

(Epictetus, *Discourses* 1.18.1–10, paraphrase by Bonforte 1974, 154)

Again, we meet with the Stoic principle that we are in fact immune from harm, and that the bad person, in falling into vice, is really doing harm to themselves, and not to anyone else. And this being the case, Epictetus asks his students why they should get angry at the bad person, for the bad person has (without realising the truth of it) committed the crime against himself. Epictetus continues the above Discourse, saying:

> Why, then, are we angry? Because we attach such importance to the things that they take from us. So, don't attach importance to your clothes, and you are not angry with the thief. Don't attach importance to the beauty of your wife, and you are not angry with the adulterer. Know that the thief and the adulterer have no place in the things that are yours, but in those that belong to others and are not in your power. If you dismiss those things and set them at nought, with whom are you still angry? But as long as you set store by these things, be angry with yourself rather than with the thief and the adulterer.
>
> For just consider: You have beautiful clothes; your neighbour does not. You have a window, and wish to air them. He does not know what man's good consists in, but imagines that it means having beautiful clothes, the very thing that you imagine too. Then, shall he not come and carry them off? When you show a bit of food to hungry men and then gobble it down alone, don't you want them to snatch at it? Don't provoke them; don't have a window; don't air your clothes.
>
> Something similar happened to me the other day. I kept an iron lamp by my household shrine. Hearing a noise from my window, I ran down. I found the lamp had been stolen. I reasoned that the one who had lifted it had felt something he couldn't resist. So what? 'Tomorrow,' I said to myself, 'you will find one of earthenware.' For a man loses what he has.
>
> (Epictetus, *Discourses* 1.18.11–16, trans. Dobbin 1998, 37)

EXERCISES

Please continue writing your daily Journal, and for the next few weeks concentrate specifically on dealing with other people, and on dealing with 'difficult people' should you encounter any. If you make any efforts to mend their ways, make a detailed record in your Journal of what you say, how they respond, and whether your efforts make any difference or not. If there are any people with whom you do not get on very well, or with whom you have fallen out, consider the options for mending fences. Use your knowledge of Stoic ideas to counsel yourself with respect to how you might undertake such an exercise, and if it seems appropriate and the opportunities arise, try to restore friendly relations.

1. Explain why the Stoics say that 'it is not people's actions that trouble us' (*Meditations* 11.18, 'Seventh Rule').

2. Have you ever been worried by what other people think or say of you? Will your knowledge of Stoic philosophy make any difference as to how you react to other people's opinions in the future?

3. To what extent does Marcus' position as Emperor invalidate the *Meditations* as a source of advice and inspiration for its modern readers? (With reference to 11.18: ' ... how I was born to preside over them, as a ram over his flock ... ')

4. Seneca discusses the nature of friendship in Letters 3, 9 and 48 (*Letters from a Stoic*, pp. 34–6, pp. 47–52 and pp. 96–7).
   (a) What is the purpose of friendship, according to Seneca?
   (b) Do you think that your capacity for 'practising friendship' has been affected in any way by your acquaintance with Stoic philosophy?

In his book, *On Duties,* Cicero remarks that cases can arise in which expediency seems to conflict with honour. In the following thought-experiment, he asks his reader to imagine that there has been a crop-failure and that consequently a terrible famine has ravaged the island of Rhodes. What few provisions remain can be had only at enormously inflated prices. A merchant from Alexandria is aboard his ship bringing a large shipment of corn to the stricken island.

> He is aware that a number of other traders are [also] on their way from Alexandria – he has seen their ships making for Rhodes, with substantial cargoes of grain. [When he arrives,] ought he to tell the Rhodians this? Or is he to say nothing and sell his stock at the best price he can get? I am assuming he is an enlightened, honest person. I am asking you to consider the deliberations and self-searchings of the sort of man who would not keep the Rhodians in ignorance if he thought this would be dishonest but who is not certain that dishonesty would be involved.
>
> In cases of this kind that eminent and respected Stoic Diogenes of Babylon habitually takes one side, and his very clever pupil Antipater of Tarsus the other. Antipater says that all the facts must be revealed, and the purchaser must be as fully informed as the seller. According to Diogenes, on the other hand, the seller must declare the defects of his wares as far as the law of the land requires, but otherwise – provided he tells no untruths – he is entitled, as a seller of goods, to sell them as profitably as he can.
>
> 'I have brought my cargo, I have offered it for sale, I offer it as cheap as other dealers – perhaps cheaper, when I am over-stocked. Whom am I cheating?'
>
> Antipater argues on the other side. '[...] You ought to work for your fellow-men and serve the interests of mankind. These are the conditions under which you were born, these are the principles which you are duty bound to

follow and obey – you must identify your interests with the interests of the community, and theirs with yours. How, then, can you conceal from your fellow-men that abundant supplies and benefits are due to reach them shortly?'

'Concealing is one thing,' perhaps Diogenes will reply, 'but *not revealing* is another. If I do not reveal to you, at this moment, what the good are like – or the nature of the Highest Good – I am not *concealing* that information [...]. I am not obliged to tell you everything that would be useful for you to know.'

'Oh yes, you are,' Antipater will reply, 'if you remember that nature has joined mankind together in one community.'

(Cicero, *On Duties* 3.50–3 [with omissions], trans. Grant 1971, 177–8)

Cicero concludes by remarking that neither Diogenes nor Antipater is saying, 'Since this action is expedient, I will do it regardless of its being wrong.' Diogenes' position is that selling at a high price is expedient, but is not in fact wrong, whereas Antipater says that (despite its being expedient) selling at a high price would be wrong. (Diogenes of Seleucia on the Tigris in Babylon, *c.*228–140 BC, was fifth scholarch of the Stoic school and was the teacher of Antipater of Tarsus, *c.*200–*c.*130 BC, who was the sixth scholarch.)

5. Imagine that you are the merchant bringing the desperately needed corn to Rhodes. Would you keep silent about the other merchants who are also on their way, and sell your corn at the highest price you can? Or would you tell the inhabitants about the other merchants, and sell at the standard price? Explain your reasons.

Here is another case devised by Cicero:

Suppose that a good man is selling his house because of certain faults that he knows and that others do not know, say, that it is unsanitary but thought to be salubrious, or that it is not generally known that vermin can be found in all the bedrooms, or that it is structurally unsound and crumbling, but no one except the owner knows this. My question is this: if the seller does not tell the buyers these things, but sells the house at a higher price than that at which he thought he would sell it, will he not have acted unjustly or dishonestly?

'He will indeed,' Antipater claims. 'Give me an instance of "failing to show the path to someone who is lost" (something which is prohibited in Athens on pain of a public curse) if it is not this: allowing a buyer to rush into a deal and succumb through his error to being thoroughly deceived. Indeed it is more than failing to show the path; rather it is knowingly to lead someone into error.'

And Diogenes again: 'If someone has not even encouraged you to buy, surely he hasn't forced you? He advertised something that he didn't want, and you bought something you did want. If those who advertise a villa as "good and well built" are not thought to have deceived you, even though it is neither good nor methodically built, then it's much less the case for those who haven't praised their house. Where it is up to the buyer to judge, how can there be deceit on the part of the seller? Indeed, if one need not accept responsibility for everything that was actually stated, do you really think that one need do so for something that was not stated?* What is more foolish than for a seller to recount the faults of the very thing he is selling? What could be more absurd than for the auctioneer to say, "I am selling an unsanitary house"?'

(Cicero, *On Duties* 3.54–55, trans. Griffin and Atkins 1991, 120)

* [Translator's note:] Diogenes is made to allude to a provision in Roman law (*Digest* XVIII.I.43) whereby the seller is not bound by professions he makes in advertising for sale as long as the qualities claimed are such as the buyer can judge for himself.

6. Imagine that you are the vendor selling the unsanitary house. Would you tell the prospective buyer the truth about the house? As before, explain your reasons.

6

IMPERMANENCE, LOSS AND DEATH

> LORD, let me know my end,
>   and what is the measure of my days;
>   let me know how fleeting my life is.
> You have made my days a few handbreadths,
>   and my lifetime is as nothing in your sight.
> Surely everyone stands as a mere breath.
>   Surely everyone goes about like a shadow.
> Surely for nothing they are in turmoil;
>   they heap up, and do not know who will gather.
>   (Psalms, 39:4–6)[1]

A pessimist may say that the well-being and peace of mind that we seek is *in fact* beyond our grasp, that the very nature of the world at large and of the human constitution make any deep and lasting tranquillity quite impossible to attain, not because we are weak or incapable of understanding and following spiritual instruction, but because of *the way things are*. Everything in the universe is transitory; even those things that for all intents and purposes we consider will last forever, are in fact temporary. The pyramids of Giza, for instance, which are already over four thousand years old (and which, no doubt, will endure for many more millennia) are destined to be lost eventually – to be robbed away by stonemasons, to be tipped up and scattered as a new mountain range rises up under them, to be buried under a massive tide of lava, or perhaps just washed away a few grains at a time by the rain. Even the earth upon which the pyramids rest will eventually be burned up and vaporised as the sun expands into a massive red giant star towards the end of its life five billion years from now.

What then of our own lives? Against this cosmic timescale they are mere flashes, of a sort, infinitesimally brief, that manifest for but a moment, that like the world we live on are destined for destruction and oblivion. And the things around us that we bother ourselves with, the possessions that we covet (sometimes obsessively), and the possessions that we actually come to own, are almost all of them even more temporary than our own bodies. The fruits of our projects, those projects that succeed, that is, are equally impermanent: whatever we make, whatever we contribute to or establish (a marriage, a school for philosophy, a new business, etc., etc.) will soon enough cease to exist. The universe itself is hostile to human endeavour.

The pessimist therefore claims that everything is ultimately futile, because all we do is doomed to decay and destruction, that a thousand years from now (and probably much sooner) it will be as if we had never lived at all. Maybe an unconscious fear of this cosmic truth explains a great deal about human culture. Most people pursue one temporary pleasure after the other, as if all that matters is gratification, for far from showing keen awareness of their eventual demise (in the face of which the maxim, 'Enjoy what pleasures you can, while you can,' may be a plausible and, perhaps, a defensible philosophy of life), most people seem to go about their business entirely ignoring – almost wilfully – the fact of personal annihilation. It is as if almost all of us were at a children's party, where, like children, we are so absorbed in the games and the prizes and the delicious food that we have completely forgotten that before so very long the party will end and dissolve.

Maybe, for many, it is even best that they keep from their conscious thoughts all ideas about the infinitely vast stretch of future time during which they will have no existence. For many, undoubtedly, the universe is quite different from how they would ideally like it to be, and the gap between the truth and the ideal is so vast that we had best not remind them of it.

But for those of us who want to fully face the facts of impermanence and death, with the wish and the hope that we can live well and be fulfilled *despite* the nature of reality, we have already seen Stoic doctrines that will aid us. The virtues (meaning those dispositions of character by which we may live as rational, sentient and self-conscious creatures should) are the only good, and death and illness and the transient nature of things are indifferent, meaning not that we are indifferent towards them – for we prefer life to death, and health to sickness – but that we pursue our projects *despite* their outcomes being impermanent. We recognise that making things permanent is not in our power, and everything we do is done 'with reservation', which obviously must include our making and contributing to things that are destined for oblivion and decay, whether that be sooner or later. For this is how God has made the world, and we will accept the world, or even love it, as it is.

The Stoic makes a commitment to face reality and to make the attempt to live well despite the discomfort, anxiety and even terror that anticipation of things ending and people dying can produce. It is better to embrace the truth, says the Stoic, than do what many people appear to do, which is to career headlong down a path of hedonistic pursuits, which will either prove such a satisfactory distraction that thoughts of transience and death will be effectively repressed, or that such thoughts as these that do arise will be quickly dismissed by the excitement of the next purchase, outing, relationship, vacation, or what have you.

✏️ **IN YOUR JOURNAL.** To what extent do you think that pursuing the usual sorts of pleasures (new clothes, use of intoxicating drugs – alcohol and nicotine, perhaps – holidays abroad, etc., etc.) has served to distract you from or mollify disturbing thoughts about impermanence and death (your own, and others')?

Do you think the pessimist is right, that the sort of world we live in makes human life fundamentally pointless and futile, that attempting to create things (buildings, institutions, works of art, etc.) is essentially an exercise in folly?

If you have been a pessimist, has this course in Stoic philosophy made any difference to your outlook?

If you have been an optimist, can you explain how your optimism has been sustained in the light of the points raised in this paper so far? (Or is it a case pretty much of just saying, 'I try not to think about that sort of thing'?)

Can you remember your first bereavement? How did you react to it?

MARCUS ON CHANGE AND TRANSFORMATION

In his *Meditations*, Marcus Aurelius develops an outlook upon transience, saying that change and transformation are desirable and necessary, and that seeing this to be the case can promote (in part) the peace of mind that the Stoic sage claims to possess.

📖 **Read Marcus Aurelius, *Meditations* 4.42, 6.15, 7.18, 8.6, 8.18 and 11.35.**

Clearly, if change and transformation did not occur, the world as a whole could not come about, and none of the things that populate the world could ever have come into being; for coming into being is itself a transformation of one thing (or many) into a new thing. We are of course ourselves the products of transformation. In the natural process of gestation, the cells that then comprised our bodies were transformed from a single-cell embryo into a human infant – and that process of transformation has gone on ever since, as our bodies convert the food we eat into new tissues, and by generating the electro-chemical energy that is required for movement, speech and thought. Indeed, 'flux and transformation are forever renewing the world' (6.15), and the uncomfortable fact of decay and death and of the ending of things must be viewed as the way in which the universe makes it possible for new things (including us) to arise and flourish.

The Stoics and other reflective people remind themselves that we are not here for very long, and that we must not allow the fact of impermanence to depress us. No sooner have we lost our heart to a little sparrow flitting by than it has passed out of sight (6.15). We should be wary of concluding that 'losing our hearts' over anything is therefore undesirable. Epictetus reminds us that what is created by transformation is eventually 'unmade', so to speak, by transformation, but that using expressions such as 'loss' and 'death' misrepresents this process:

> Never say of anything, 'I have lost it,' but rather 'I have given it back.' Has your child died? It has been given back. Has your wife died? She has been given back. Has your land been taken from you? Well, that too has been

given back. 'But the one who took it from me is a bad man!' What concern is it of yours by whose hand the Giver* asks for its return? For the time that these things are given to you, take care of them as things that belong to another, just as travellers do an inn.
(Epictetus, *Handbook* 11, trans. Seddon 2005, 65)

> * [Note:] 'The Giver' ('*ho dotêr*') is the source from which everything we have and enjoy originates, and to whom everything, eventually, must be given back. We may think of this as God, providence, fate, or nature, expressions which the Stoics understood signified one and the same thing.

There is every reason to engage fully with whatever providence brings our way. But as Stoics we do this in full acceptance that everything is transitory and will one day be 'given back', that our engaging with things should be viewed from the wider perspective in which we are each contributing to the ceaseless unfolding of the world's history.

MARCUS' NOTION OF A COSMIC PERSPECTIVE

Adopting a 'cosmic perspective' is an important aspect of Marcus' philosophy. In ordinary life, it is both natural and inevitable that we should be concerned about our own affairs and about the things, people and events that have a direct bearing on our projects. But Marcus suggests that we should place these concerns in a wider context, for when we do so, the way that we relate to those concerns subtly alters.

> **Read Marcus Aurelius, *Meditations* 5.23, 6.36, 7.48, 9.30, 10.17 and 12.32.**

When we recognise the rapidity with which things come into being only to be swept away into oblivion, and appreciate how tiny our own lives are in comparison with the thousands of years that comprise human history, or with the millions of years that comprise the history of life on earth (12.32), we begin to get a sense of how foolish we make ourselves by getting so deeply concerned about the ups and downs of daily life, as if our 'troubles would endure for any great while' (5.23).

If we adopt a cosmic perspective and look down on human affairs from a 'point far above' (7.48; 9.30) we can see everything going on at once, and the actions and concerns of any one person (who may be us) look, if not wholly trivial, then of no great importance. What would we say to the ant in the midst of a scurrying column of millions who looked up at us and declared: 'Woe am I! My little bit of leaf has fallen in the mud and is lost forever!'? If we could answer, we would want to say that that sentiment has somehow missed the true significance of what is really going on. So the next time we drop our eggs outside the supermarket, break a plate, or suffer a break-in, we should recall the talking ant, and realise that what has happened has essentially no significance whatever.

No wonder the Stoics were accused of offering a harsh philosophy, for they say that *all our misfortunes* should be regarded like the ant's little bit of leaf being lost in the mud. But the Stoics are right to point out that we bewail the ordinary and the common thing – whatever grieves us has happened to others millions of times, and we have known all along either that this very thing *must* eventually happen, or was more than likely to happen. The overall point of attempting to adopt the cosmic perspective is to gain confidence in seeing the world's history, and our own affairs within that history, *objectively*.

The way we *subjectively* experience things happening as they inevitably must can be changed to one of calm acceptance through the mental exercise of adopting an *objective*, cosmic perspective. Logically, we do not need to employ this exercise, for we already know that the things that trouble us, even major catastrophes (personal or collective) are in fact *indifferents* that are 'dispreferred'; to be sure, they disrupt our projects and are inconveniences *for them*, whereas we ourselves as agents who engage in those projects cannot be harmed. But the cosmic perspective exercise is useful because it helps us to challenge the values – that loss is truly bad, and death is supremely bad – instilled in us by society as we grew up, which, tragically and inevitably leads almost all people at one time or another into experiencing not only frustration and anxiety, but also abject misery and soul-destroying despair.[2]

 📖 Read Marcus Aurelius, *Meditations* 12.27.

SEEING THINGS AS THEY TRULY ARE

Epictetus and Marcus encourage a further exercise for strengthening an objective viewpoint. They urge us to be strictly honest and accurate in the way we describe things.

 📖 Read Marcus Aurelius, *Meditations* 3.11, 6.13, 8.21 and 12.8.

If we practise this exercise of stopping to 'see what sort of thing' (8.21) we are dealing with, we should find it much more easy to 'act with reservation' and not be so easily surprised at the way things turn out. We can apply this exercise as much to people as to anything else: some people are selfish and act for themselves; others are kindly and considerate to others; some are timid and are uncomfortable with others, or in new situations; and some face a daily battle with anxiety even in a daily routine that is wholly familiar, in contrast with others who are always confident no matter what. We cannot expect anything other than that people will behave in accord with their temperaments, even if we have reasons to hope that they will not! With respect to the things around us and the events that occur as part of ordinary life, it is perhaps even easier for us to 'see them as they truly are' (6.13) and thereby stand a better chance of retaining our equanimity instead of falling into some unnecessary emotion such as rage or frustration, annoyance or disappointment.

If we drop and break something, well, this has happened because it is in the nature of the human constitution sometimes to be clumsy, and it is in the nature of the broken item to break. If we lose a gold ring, for example, we should say that it is a little piece of metal that we have lost, and well, it is in the nature of small things to be easily lost.

If someone tries to impress us with the size of their office or the size of their house, we should think only that they have a large carpet to pace up and down on, or that they have a large number of rooms they can look into. If they wear expensive clothes to show how better than us they are, we should think only that the cloth with which they cover their bodies has been charged at a higher price. If someone marvels at a tremendously expensive painting, say only that they marvel at a piece of canvas with some pigment daubed onto it, with a price tag having more zeros on it than others: whether the painting is competently made, well, that is another question.

> With respect to any of those things you find attractive or useful or have a fondness for, recall to mind what kind of thing it is, beginning with the most trifling. So if you are fond of an earthenware pot, say, 'I am fond of an earthenware pot.' Then you will not be upset if it gets broken. When you kiss your child or wife, say that you are kissing

a human being; then, should they die, you will not be distressed.
   (Epictetus, *Handbook* 3, trans. Seddon 2005, 44–5)

Clearly, Epictetus is applying the same 'see what sort of thing this is' exercise as we have just been discussing and, equally clearly, many people would find his final sentence distasteful if not appalling. To lose someone we are close to is the worst possible of human misfortunes, and to suggest that we should adopt an outlook that will prevent us from being upset seems to be suggesting that we should strive to be less than human, for how can it be said that we really loved someone if we are not upset at losing them? The Stoic, as we know, would refute that charge, and claim, paradoxically, that it is people who get carried away by events and who get upset by losses who fall short of their potential humanity.

Our task here is to accept, if we can, that it is better not to be dominated by circumstances beyond our control, that it is undesirable that our emotions should be directed by the actions of others and by the unfolding of events generally, or, in particular, by life taking its own inevitable journey terminating in death.

The philosophers in all the ancient schools claimed to be able to relieve us of our fear of death (with respect to our own ending, and to the ending of others), for philosophy was conceived of as a therapy that can cure us of our fears and unwanted passions, and of our misconceptions, whether or not they lead to such fears and passions. Accordingly, the Stoics addressed the topic of death and, as you may have already noticed, it is a topic that frequently appears in Marcus' *Meditations*. We will return to Marcus later, but for the moment we will look to see how Seneca responds to the question of finding a therapy for coping with loss and grief.

THE STOICS AND THE FEAR OF DEATH

The 'consolation', a text designed to comfort and to alleviate the grief of those who have suffered a major loss, originated in the earliest Greek poetry. By the time Seneca and Marcus Aurelius were writing, the consolation had developed into a specialised literary form, examples of which would draw on traditionally accepted lists of topics (not all available topics being necessarily employed in any one consolation), and not infrequently the author sets out merely to 'remind' their reader that such-and-such is the case, to reinforce an outlook or belief that has been temporarily shaken by the shock of their loss.

The consolation is by no means the unique preserve of Stoic philosophers, for the genre was invented and developed long before the founding of the Stoic school. It is not even the unique preserve of philosophers, though philosophers of all persuasions drew on it freely, for poets, writers and rhetoricians all used the consolation in their work when they wished. The consolation as a literary genre would have been familiar to all educated people in the Graeco-Roman world, whether they ever encountered Stoic versions or not.

> Read Seneca, *Letters from a Stoic*, Letter 63, pp. 113–17.

This letter offers us an example of the consolation. Lucilius' friend, Flaccus, has died, and Seneca is writing with the intention that Lucilius should not 'grieve unduly over' his friend's death.

Although Seneca is convinced that it is best not to grieve at all, he recognises that Lucilius will fall short of this ideal. Even the Stoic sage who has been 'lifted far out of fortune's reach' by shaping his character through Stoic practice will nevertheless 'feel a twinge of pain'. For those of us making progress towards the ideal of sagehood, giving way to tears is pardonable so long as our grief is not excessive. Seneca believes that we should strike a mean, and our 'eyes should be neither dry nor streaming' (p. 114).

> ✎ **IN YOUR JOURNAL. Read Letter 63 again, and carefully distinguish the points that Seneca musters in his effort to reduce Lucilius' grief.**

(1) We must be careful to recognise the possibility that in giving way to grief we are merely trying to prove to ourselves and others that we feel our loss. As we have seen, the Stoics are concerned to point out that in giving way to excessive emotions, we are feeling and displaying not just our sense of loss, but just as significantly, we are representing to ourselves the situation we face in a *seriously flawed and distorted way*. Seneca is especially worried that we should not parade our grief (p. 114).

(2) These points constitute an assault upon the validity of the depth of Lucilius' grief. They ought to at least make him pause and attempt to make a more objective assessment of his loss and his reaction to it.

(3) We must not confuse grieving for our loss with keeping a lost friend in our memories. Our memories that commemorate and celebrate a lost friend will endure long after our grief has subsided (p. 114).

(4) Indeed, our memories of lost friends ought to be a pleasure for us (pp. 114–15).

(5) Fortune gives as well as takes away. We should make the most of friends while we have them, 'since no one can tell how long we shall have the opportunity' (p. 115). If our loss deprives us of our only friend 'we

have done ourselves a greater injury than fortune has done us' (p. 115), for fortune has deprived us of just this one friend, whereas we are to blame for depriving ourselves of 'every friend we have failed to make' (p. 115).

(6) The upshot is that we should not waste our energies in excessive grieving, but should set out to make good our loss, and find a new friend.

(7) Everyone will find an end to their grief 'in the passing of time' (p. 116). This is perhaps an exaggeration, for there are bound to be some individuals for whom the loss of someone close to them produces a permanent effect, for whom the world takes on a different aspect now that the person they loved is no longer a part of the world. In such cases, Stoic therapy may at least help such a person to face the world in its new aspect, promote the taking up of worthwhile projects, and transform a long-term debilitating grief into one that can be managed.

(8) Persisting in grief can sour our relationships, and even make us look ridiculous (pp. 116–17).

Seneca concludes his consolation by freely admitting his own faults: he says that he was himself 'defeated by grief' when his friend Annaeus Serenus died. The reason for this was his entirely ignoring the possibility that his friend might die before him because he was so young, and Seneca was that much older (p. 117). Seneca is saying essentially that because he is older than his friend, he should expect his friend to outlive him 'with reservation'. It is reasonable to expect his friend to outlive him, but foolish to expect it with certainty.

We need to remind ourselves that inevitably everyone will soon enough perish, including ourselves, that loss of all sorts, and bereavement in particular, is the lot of human beings. By rehearsing our losses, by recognising what they are likely to be, or what assuredly they must be, *by expecting them*, we will be better able to cope with the emotional blows that will undoubtedly fall upon us (see Letter 26, last paragraph, pp. 71–2).

FACING OUR OWN DEPARTURE FROM LIFE

We are each of us guests, temporarily residing on a planet that is itself temporary. Where we came from and whither we shall go once we die – and whether that question even makes sense – we will never know with certainty. But what we can be certain of is that our stay here is limited (and for some that stay is regarded as being pitifully brief), and that soon enough our experiences of this world will cease forever. Human beings are fated to have an awareness of their own mortality. As you may have noticed, Marcus is deeply troubled by this fact, and he uses a large number of his meditations to address the question of how he can maintain his spirits and live well in the face of his certain knowledge about his own mortality.

 Read Marcus Aurelius, *Meditations* 2.11.

Marcus reminds us of the key Stoic doctrine that it is impossible to fall into genuine evil, for the only true evil is vice, and we are equipped with a rationality, or the potential for such, that will keep us from vice if we are determined to achieve such an end. That same rationality will also direct us to virtue, the only good. Which makes death and our fear of death 'indifferent' things. In short, fearing death as a bad thing is not possible, because death is not bad. The Stoics claim, therefore, that those who fear death have made a mistake, and that really there is nothing fearful there at all.

Marcus locates his discussion firmly within a wider theological analysis, and we may be more or less sympathetic to his views, here. Either way, it can be argued that regardless of what the theological facts may be, it remains the case that only virtue is good, vice is bad, and that indifferent things – including the fact of death and the fear of death – if properly understood, cannot disturb our peace of mind: for if these indifferent things 'cannot make a person worse in himself' then they cannot 'make his life worse', either. (For more of this theological analysis, see, for example, *Meditations* 12.5.)

> 📖 Read Marcus Aurelius, *Meditations* 6.2, 6.47 and 8.5.

Our task is to 'make good use of what the moment brings' (6.2), to use whatever arises as the material upon which we exercise our capacity for virtuous action, 'to pass our days in truth and justice' (6.47). Marcus reminds himself that the fact of death cannot prevent him from keeping his 'eyes fixed on the matter in hand' and cannot diminish his 'duty to be a good person' (8.5).

> 📖 Read Marcus Aurelius, *Meditations* 9.3 and 9.21.

Chapter 9.3 reiterates Marcus' views of change, transformation and death, emphasising the point that death is a natural process, and for this reason is a fact of life that we can actually welcome. (For more on death as a process of nature, see 2.12, 4.5 and 11.34; and for this process not being within our control, see 5.33.) A rather interesting argument is presented in 9.21. Here Marcus points out that in considering our lives in terms of their various stages, of childhood, adolescence, early adulthood, and so on, we should notice that our childhood, for instance, has now ended and that the shift to 'each change is a death'; for the moving from one stage to the next will necessitate 'many losses, alterations, and cessations'. Each stage is complete in itself. If someone should die just as they are entering adolescence, their childhood stage was all the same settled, complete and finished, having just the characteristics that it in fact had, being filled with all those events that actually happened, no less than had this person lived on into old age. A reflective adolescent may fear death and worry that their adolescence will end. Marcus would ask: 'Why do you fear the losses, alterations, and cessations that death would bring – because those losses will occur anyway, even if you live for eighty more years?'

Seneca makes a similar observation:

> Every day we die, for every day part of our life is lost, and even when we are growing bigger our life is growing shorter. We have lost successively childhood, boyhood, youth. Right up to yesterday all the time which has passed has been lost, and this present day itself we share with death. It is not the last drop of water which empties the water-clock, but all that dripped out previously. In the same way the final hour when we actually die does not alone bring our death but simply completes the process. At that point we have arrived at death, but we have been journeying thither for a long time.
> (Seneca, *Moral Letters* 24.20, trans. Costa 1988, 27)

📖 **Read Marcus Aurelius, *Meditations* 2.14 and 3.10.**

Marcus' overall thesis is that death cannot actually deprive us of anything. Events that lie in the future and which we suppose we will eventually come to experience, are not yet in our possession, and this being so means that we cannot now be deprived of them. Clearly, we have a tendency to imagine ourselves occupying our own futures when we have no entitlement to do so.

> 📖 Read Marcus Aurelius, *Meditations* 12.35 and 12.36.

At least as important as the points already made is the idea that we can have no complaints when nature, who brought us into the world, so arranges events that we are led out again. The Stoic accepts this situation and abides by the rules set down by nature (or God, or fate). For what can *not accepting* this ever amount to, except lamenting and bewailing that which cannot be changed?

To be sure, the Stoic views their own death as the release they are entitled to, having done their best to live a good life in the service of God.

> Just as on a voyage, when the ship has anchored, if you go ashore to get water you may also pick up a shell-fish or a vegetable from the path, but you should keep your thoughts fixed on the ship, and you should look back frequently in case the captain calls, and, if he should call, you must give up all these other things to avoid being bound and thrown on board like a sheep; so in life also, if instead of a vegetable and a shell-fish you are given a wife and a child, nothing will prevent you from taking them – but if the captain calls, give up all these things and run to the ship without even turning to look back. And if you are old, do not even go far from the ship, lest you are missing when the call comes.
>
> (Epictetus, *Handbook* 7, trans. Seddon 2005, 56)

Life is merely stepping ashore briefly on a strange land where we will occupy ourselves for a short time before the captain calls us back to the boat, and we must depart. If we are unwilling to leave, we will be tied up like livestock and thrown into the boat anyway.[3] The captain, of course, is God, or fate, or nature. We should always bear in mind that whatever we do, however we occupy ourselves, is only a temporary business; we should 'look round frequently in case the captain calls'. All that we have, as we have seen, is merely on loan, and nothing is truly our own. We must be ready to leave everything the moment we are summoned.

CONCLUDING THOUGHTS

Where has our exploration of Stoic philosophy taken us, I wonder? For some, these teachings will make a real difference to our living well, in good spirits, despite life's vicissitudes. Others, for whom these teachings look mistaken or ludicrous, will be disappointed and frustrated, and may even despair of finding a philosophical or spiritual path that will effectively address their concerns. But such a path – wherever it may lie – is surely one that leads to some kind of deep insight or enlightenment.

And just as surely, enlightenment, or spiritual transformation, is not something that happens *to you*, rather it is something that you do *for yourself* by coming to see things differently – it is a process in which you both come to see things differently, and in which *seeing things this way makes more sense*. From within a new 'enlightened' perspective, a range of previously unconnected items now cohere into a meaningful picture; things have a different significance, in consequence of which you will relate to people and things and events in the world at large in new ways. Put most simply, spiritual transformation is an awakening to the truth. When the Stoics speak of themselves 'making progress', it is towards such a truth, as they conceive it, that they strive to advance. If Stoic teaching has spoken to you on this level, then you have already made progress, and you will be able to continue to make progress.

But if this is not the case, at least you have the satisfaction of knowing that the Stoic path to transformation is not your path. You may even have had some insight into why this is so and what sorts of features you need to look for in 'your own' spiritual path – and this insight may enable you to find what you are seeking that bit more easily.

If you have had no such insights, and for you the picture is even more bleak, you have no option but to continue the search nevertheless. The curiosity or disquiet, or even desperation that encouraged you to take up these studies must now be deployed in the examination of other paths. My own search, for what it is worth, took over twenty years, and my efforts to 'make progress' as a Stoic are of course ongoing, and it is quite doubtful that there is any terminus at which this work can ever be deemed complete.

> **Read Marcus Aurelius, *Meditations* 4.49 and 12.13.**

EXERCISES

You will know by now whether writing your Journal has proved an asset or an inconvenience without any real benefit. If you find journal-writing helpful, please continue to write your Journal. There are numerous books on the topic of journal-writing, and you may be interested to explore this exercise further once you have concluded working on this course.

There are a greater number of questions to conclude this paper than in previous papers. The opening questions address the topic of death discussed in Paper 6, the other questions are included to guide you in a basic revision of key Stoic concepts (and thereby constitute a revision of the whole course), and the final question is for self-assessment. Please write responses to all the questions marked with an asterisk*, and of the remaining six questions, please write responses to at least three (or more, if you like). Choose the optional questions carefully because, as you will see, there is a fair degree of overlap, and it is probably wise to address a wider, rather than a narrower, range of topics.

*1. Does the Stoic approach to death console you when contemplating (a) your own death, or (b) the deaths of your friends and relatives? Explain your answer.

*2. Does it *matter* that human life is transitory?

*3. Why do the Stoics regard living a life as a 'stopover at an inn'? (Seneca, note 2, below; and Epictetus, *Handbook* 11, quoted above.)

4. Explain what the Stoics mean when they say that all that we have is merely 'on loan'.

*5. Either
    (a) Explain what the Stoics mean by the expression 'indifferent'. Give some examples of preferred indifferents and dispreferred indifferents. Explain *why* they are preferred or dispreferred.
    or
    (b) What does Epictetus means when he says that some things are in our power and some things are not? Explain how he uses this idea in his overall presentation of Stoic philosophy.

6. Explain what the Stoic is trying to do when they 'act with reservation'.

7. Explain the Stoic motto, 'Live according to nature.'

8. Seneca, in particular, emphasises the need to live simply. Why?

9. Explain the Stoic exercise of 'self-examination'.

10. Explain the Stoic concept of God.

11. Explain why the Stoic does not get angry with other people.

*12. Either
  (a) What is being claimed when the Stoic student says that they are 'making progress'? Making progress towards *what*?
  or
  (b) What are the ills that Stoic philosophy is supposed to cure?

*13. Epictetus says of someone making progress, that ' ... he keeps watch over himself as over an enemy lying in ambush' (*Enchiridion* 48, trans. Higginson 1944, p. 350). What exactly are they watching *for*?

*14. Please write a short self-assessment of your experience of doing this course (300 words, approximately). Do you feel that you have benefited from it? Has it changed your life in any way? Do you feel that the Stoic approach for coping with life's adversities has been of benefit to you, and will it help you cope with troubles you personally may face? You may begin your assessment by stating either:
  (a) Since making this study of Stoic philosophy my outlook on life has changed because ...
  or
  (b) Despite being introduced to Stoic philosophy my outlook on life has not changed because ...

NOTES

1. The Scripture quotation contained herein is from the New Revised Standard Version Bible, copyright, 1989, by the Division of Christian Education of the National Council of Churches of Christ in the USA. Used by permission. All rights reserved.
2. Seneca also urges adopting a cosmic perspective in his consolation to Marcia, whose son has died:

   > Born for the briefest time, soon to yield to one's replacement, we regard this as a stopover at an inn. Am I speaking about our life, which whirls along with incredible velocity? Compute the ages of cities: you will see how even those which boast their antiquity have not stood for a long time. All human affairs are short-lived and perishable, comprising no portion of infinite time. When compared with the universe, we reckon this earth with its cities, its populace, its rivers, its surrounding sea as minute; if life be compared to all of time, its portion is less than minute.
   > (Seneca, *To Marcia* 21.1-2, trans. Motto and Clark 1993, 43)

3. In Chapter 3.3 of the *Meditations*, Marcus reverses this metaphor and sees life as a voyage, and death as coming into port at the end of the voyage.

APPENDIX 1

DO THE STOICS SUCCEED IN SHOWING HOW PEOPLE CAN BE MORALLY RESPONSIBLE FOR SOME OF THEIR ACTIONS WITHIN THE FRAMEWORK OF CAUSAL DETERMINISM?

The Stoic teachers exhort their students to pursue the correct moral path. Seneca urges Lucilius to become a philosopher, and to live life *as* a philosopher, saying:

> It is clear to you, I know, Lucilius, that no one can lead a happy life, or even one that is bearable, without the pursuit of wisdom, and that the perfection of wisdom is what makes the happy life, although even the beginning of wisdom makes life bearable.
> (*Moral Letters* 16.1, Campbell 1969, 63)

It would be futile to instruct someone to do something that is known to be impossible. How silly is would be for Stoic teachers to urge their students to exercise their capacity for free will, to choose the correct moral path, if all along it is known that it never is in anyone's power to do one thing rather than another.

THE CAUSAL THEORY OF DETERMINISM

The Stoics hold that all events throughout the course of history are every one connected to antecedent events that cause them, and that they in turn are themselves antecedent causes of what must follow after. This is the theory of causal determinism. Events occur when they do because they are caused by prior events, and these events were caused to occur when they did by events yet more prior – and so on all the way back to the beginning of the world. And all the way *forward* to the end of the world. According to this theory, there never has been and there never will be even a single event that is not caused. Everything is how it is, whenever it is how it is, because it has been determined to be like that by prior circumstances that cause it. Events on the thread of time are not like beads on a thread: the first bead may be red, the second blue, and the third green. But the blue bead is not blue *because* the first one is red, and the green bead is not green *because* the second bead is blue. Events in time are different. So long as we identify the events correctly, we *can* say that event B occurs *because of* event A, and that event C occurs *because of* event B. Stobaeus tells us that:

> Zeno says that a cause is 'that because of which' – [and] Chrysippus says [also] that a cause is 'that because of which' ... while that of which it is the cause is 'why?'
> (Stobaeus 1.138,14–139,4, Long and Sedley 1987, 55A, p. 333)

The entire sequence of causes which stretches out to form the entire history of the world was called by the ancients, fate. Cicero has his speaker say in defence of the Stoic theory of divination:

> By 'fate' I mean what the Greeks call *heimarmenê* – an ordering and sequence of causes, since it is the connexion of cause to cause which out of itself produces anything. ... Consequently nothing has happened which was not going to be, and likewise nothing is going to be of which nature does not contain causes working to bring that very thing about. This makes it intelligible that fate should be, not the

'fate' of superstition, but that of physics, an everlasting cause of things — why past things happened, why present things are now happening, and why future things will be.
(Cicero, *On Divination* 1.125–6, Long and Sedley 1987, 55L, p. 337)

But if the whole history of the world is exactly and precisely an enormously complex mass of causal threads juxtaposed and interconnected, such that any event and every event embedded in this unimaginably vast nexus *must* be how it is, where it is, and when it is, how might someone do something different, do A, say, which is morally preferable, rather than B, which is in some measure morally reprehensible? For if the theory of causal determinism is true, no one can ever choose to do A rather than B, or B rather than A. No one ever chooses to do anything. If the Stoic teacher tells the pupil to do A, and they do, this was all along fated to occur. And if they were told to do A, and they do B, then it was *this* that was all along fated.

If the Stoics are right, and everything is fated to occur just as it does, how can it make sense for them to believe that we are free agents, able to choose what to do, responsible for our own actions, praiseworthy or blameworthy depending on the rightness of our action? Why bother to aim at anything at all? If a certain event A has been fated to occur for all time, why worry about trying to bring A about? It will happen whatever I do. More foolish would be my trying to prevent A. Were I to try, I would fail.

THE 'LAZY ARGUMENT' AND CO-FATED EVENTS

The fatalist can reply that this is not right. Should the theory of causal determinism be true, and should fate thereby be a fact concerning the world, it does not follow that acting is never to any avail. The thought that action *is* never to any avail is expressed in the 'Lazy Argument', and 'If we gave in to it,' says Cicero, 'we would do nothing whatever in life.'

> [The argument is posed] as follows: 'If it is your fate to recover from this illness, you will recover, regardless of whether or not you call the doctor. Likewise, if it is your fate not to recover from this illness, you will not recover, regardless of whether or not you call the doctor. And one or the other *is* your fate. Therefore it is pointless to call the doctor.'
> (Cicero, *On Fate* 28, Long and Sedley 1987, 55S, p. 339)

Cicero continues, saying that Chrysippus criticised this argument. Some events are complex and 'co-fated'. It is false that you will recover from the illness whether or not you call the doctor, because your calling the doctor, and having some treatment, may be the reason why you recover. Calling the doctor, and recovering, are 'co-fated'. So, to take action certainly can be effective – your calling the doctor resulting in your recovery.

Though seeing this doesn't to any degree undermine the fatalist's position, for just as your recovering was fated (if only you had known it), so was your calling the doctor! This might be how it happened, all right, but if the event of your calling the doctor was caused by prior circumstances (as all events are, according to the theory of causal determinism) then in what sense could you be considered to exercise your free will?

CHRYSIPPUS' CYLINDER

Chrysippus employs the example of a cylinder made to roll down a hill (Cicero, *On fate* 42–3 = Long and Sedley 62C8–9, pp. 386–8; Aulus Gellius, *Attic nights* 7.2.11 = Long and

Sedley 62D4, pp. 388–9). He says that there are two distinct types of cause working here. One is our *pushing* the cylinder to make it move; this is the 'auxiliary and proximate cause' – we can call it the 'external cause'. And the other is the cylinder's *being round*; this is the 'complete and primary cause' – which we can call the 'internal cause' (see Long and Sedley 62C5-6, p. 387). We may be inclined to object that the *being round* is not really a cause. It is a property that the cylinder has, as would be its redness and heaviness, just in case it is red and heavy. Chrysippus could reply, and say that whereas the colour and weight of the cylinder have no bearing on its rolling – a blue, light cylinder rolls just as well – its *roundness* does have a bearing on its rolling: if it weren't round, it wouldn't roll. We would say that the roundness was a *necessary condition* for the cylinder's rolling, just as the pushing of the cylinder was also necessary: no push, no rolling. But together both the roundness and the pushing were sufficient for the rolling. Chrysippus wants us to note that both the external cause and the internal cause themselves had causes properly located in the causal nexus comprising the entire history of the world. The external cause of the push was itself caused by our foot swinging to meet the cylinder, and the internal cause of the cylinder's roundness was caused by the manufacturing process that made it. And we may suppose that the *rolling* will itself cause something else to happen, such as the knocking over of a sheep, or a splash in the stream, or both. In short, nothing has happened which violates the theory of causal determinism.

INTERNAL CAUSES AND HUMAN AGENCY

Next we must apply the logical structure of this example to the case of a human agent. Consider someone who sees a cake on a table. The Stoics talk of perception in terms of 'assenting' to an 'impression'. Having got an impression of a cake, which is to say that the agent's mind has been causally altered by the cake – just in case there really is a cake on the table, but otherwise causally altered by something else that makes it *seem* that there is a cake on the table – the agent is ready to 'assent' to this impression: which is to say, the agent can say, 'Yes. It is true that there is a cake on the table.' For Chrysippus, the impression is like the *push* given to the cylinder. Just as the push was necessary, but not sufficient, for the cylinder's rolling, the impression was necessary, but not sufficient, for the agent's assenting to it. The impression is an external cause. The *internal* cause of the assent (necessary and with the impression jointly sufficient for the assent) is the agent's own nature, corresponding to the nature of the cylinder's roundness. The agent's nature then, comprises 'the power of impulse and repulsion, of desire and avoidance – in a word, the power of using impressions' (Epictetus, *Discourses* 1.1.12, trans. Dobbin 1998, 3).

A human agent is *not* like a billiard ball, which if struck *must* move off in a certain direction at a certain speed. When 'struck' by an impression, the agent can decide what to do, can decide to assent to it, and can decide what to do next. But just as the cylinder's roundness had antecedent causes so that its being like that fitted in to the overall causal nexus of fate, so too does the agent's nature have antecedent causes, these being the agent's upbringing, attending the classes of a Stoic teacher, and what have you. So again, the theory of causal determinism is unviolated – *and* it is 'up to' the agent, and 'in their power' to assent to impressions and to act as they see fit. If this has all been argued correctly, Chrysippus *can* have his cake and eat it: that is, causal determinism is true, *and* agents can exercise their free will.

But to what extent *is* the agent free to form their own nature? If their nature is something that is just imposed on them, how can they be said to be free when this nature determines the outcome of their dealings with circumstance? If through the workings of fate they are exposed to just these experiences, acquire these skills, and develop this particular personality, it would appear to be 'up to' *fate* that they react as they do under the influence of some impression. Internal causes, our own natures, our own dispositions, appear to be locked into and determined in their character by the causal nexus of fate as much as external causes are. Chrysippus is right to draw the distinction between these two kinds of cause, but doing so, and elaborating the distinction, does not help us locate human freedom within a fully determined world.

INDETERMINISM

Would it be better, then, to reject the theory of causal determinism, and to say that at least some events are *uncaused*, to say that at least some events do *not* have antecedent conditions, causally necessary and sufficient for their coming about? That is, they just happen anyway. They happen, and there just is no explanation for their happening. This would be to embrace some type of indeterminism. But we can see immediately that this option is unhelpful and probably rather silly. For where do we locate human freedom in such an undetermined, if only partly undetermined, world? Two options may be entertained. Either I reach for the cake, and my action is causally determined by necessary antecedent external causes (my seeing the cake) and by necessary internal causes (my own nature, my predispositions to reach out for something edible in this sort of circumstance) which are jointly sufficient for my acting as I do – *or* my reaching for the cake is entirely *uncaused*: my arm just shoots out for no reason at all, my hand grabs the cake, and the next instant that same hand is stuffing the cake into my mouth, all of this for no reason at all, for an uncaused event or action by definition has no explanation of any kind.

Far from allowing freedom to occur, the notion of uncaused events makes my acting to a purpose of my own free will *impossible*.

OUR OWN EXPERIENCE AS AGENTS

We might do better to consider how we experience events on a moment-to-moment, day by day basis. It certainly *seems* to us that we are not always caused to act as we do directly by circumstances around us, and it does *seem* that it is up to us, in some measure at least, as to how we develop and train our inner dispositions – which like the roundness of the cylinder *do* play an important part in our responding to and dealing with affairs in the world. Indeed, the whole of Stoic moral philosophy has the purpose of bringing our inner dispositions into line with living in such a way as to exhibit moral virtue and living well in the way the Stoics conceive of doing this.

I am not *made* to eat the cake just because I see it. If I eat the cake, I do so deliberately. I may take time to deliberate about whether or not to eat the cake, or I may not. Either way, my eating the cake is a deliberate act, and what I do deliberately I do freely. Of course there are influences – causal influences – at work here. My feeling hungry, if I do, clearly influences my decision to eat the cake. But this is exactly how I want matters to be. My action only *makes sense* if these influences are present.

STOIC THEOLOGY

There is one argument that the Stoics may well have offered when confronted with the apparent paradox of human freedom being allowed within the causal nexus of fate. None of the ancient sources express this argument, but since it seems to be implied by and is consistent with their theology, they would have been able to employ it had they wished (see Long 1996b, 178–80).

The Stoics identified *logos* (reason), fate and god, regarding them as different aspects of the one principle which creates and sustains the world (see Diogenes Laertius 7.134–5 = Long and Sedley 1987, 44B and 46B, pp. 268–9, 275). God, through acting on passive unqualified substance, makes it what it is. But since god is considered to be a *body*, and is coextensive with the world and is 'in' everything, god must also be in *us*. The Stoics believed that the governing part of each human soul, the *hêgemonikon*, is a fragment of the divine *logos*. Epictetus imagines Zeus talking to him: 'I have given you a part of myself, the power of impulse and repulsion, of desire and avoidance – in a word, the power of using impressions' (*Discourses* 1.1.12, Dobbin 1998, 3). Later, he writes:

> For if god had so arranged his own part, which he has given to us as a fragment of himself, that it would be hindered or constrained by himself or by anyone else, he would no longer be god, nor would he be caring for us as he ought.
> (Epictetus, *Discourses* 1.17.27, Dobbin 1998, 36)

It would be wrong, therefore, to regard Stoic fate as being external to agents, as a force that operates *upon* them. Rather, we should view fate as operating *through* agents. We are partners with god, working *with* god to bring about the history of the world as it is meant to be brought about. Should we find ourselves reacting to circumstances in this way rather than that, this is not necessarily fate compelling an outcome that has been predestined behind our backs so to speak; it may be that we ourselves are of our own free volition and in some very small measure, making fate into what it is.

APPENDIX 2

THE STOICS ON WHY WE SHOULD STRIVE TO BE FREE OF THE PASSIONS

Like the other schools of the Hellenistic period, the Stoics held that the correct end (*telos*) for human beings is 'happiness' (*eudaimonia*) or 'living well' (*eu zên*). None of the schools accepted this in a descriptive sense: it is not the case that people have an in-built capacity for doing what is required for living well. The Hellenistic schools, including the Stoic school, took it upon themselves to supply their own normative accounts of what we *ought to do* to live well.

In the briefest of outlines, the Stoic theory held that the only good thing is virtue (*aretê*, 'excellence of character') and the only bad thing is vice, its opposite. Everything else is 'indifferent' between virtue and vice, being in no sense at all good or bad. Thus the Stoics maintained that the bulk of humanity, in pursuing wealth and material goods, status, health and anything at all that is popularly conceiving of as good is making a mistake so long as that pursuit is based on the belief that these things really are good, or are desirable because they are good. Living virtuously is necessary and sufficient for living well and being happy, and the 'indifferent' things, although worth pursuing to the extent that it is appropriate for human beings to seek adequate shelter, sustenance and companionship, are in no way *required* for *eudaimonia*.

The Stoic view of the indifferent things goes back to Plato (see *Meno* 87c–89a and *Euthydemus* 278e–281e). If we accept that what is good must benefit us unconditionally, we can see that conventional goods fail this standard. Wealth, for example, is not unconditionally beneficial, since someone who possesses it might use it to accomplish harmful or shameful ends. And so with all the other conventional goods. Benefit results, when it does, from using conventional goods properly, and to use these things properly we need to be guided by the virtues, for it is only a character possessed of excellence that has the capacity to use conventional goods in a way that is guaranteed to benefit. If someone uses conventional goods beneficially, and does this without having an excellent character, they have done no more than achieve a fluke. Thus, it is the possession of an excellent character that benefits its possessor unconditionally, and is both necessary and sufficient for living well; and such a person will display the four traditional 'primary' virtues of temperance, justice, courage and wisdom. In all circumstances and at all times, when it is appropriate, such a person will act with self-restraint, will be just towards others, will face difficult or painful situations with courage, and will choose their activities and carry them out wisely.

One striking feature that the Stoic wise person will display, and which is necessary to their enjoying *eudaimonia*, is a character wholly *apathês*, 'without passion'. I propose now to discuss this notion of *apatheia*, and to consider exactly why the Stoic wise person must aim to attain it, and what they can do practically to attain it.

In Stoic theory there are four primary passions (*pathê*): desire (*epithumia*) is an impulse towards some anticipated thing regarded as good; fear (*phobos*) is an impulse away from some anticipated thing regarded as bad. The other two *pathê* are: delight (*hêdonê*), an impulse towards some present thing regarded as good, and distress (*lupê*), an impulse away from some present thing regarded as bad (see Long and Sedley 1987, 65A–B, pp. 410–11). Other passions are classified under these four primary passions. Anger, sexual desire, and love of riches for instance, are types of desire (Long and Sedley 1987, 65E, p. 412). The Stoics explain the passions in terms of the judgements we make regarding the circumstances we find ourselves in. Thus, the distress that someone may feel when confronted by a vicious animal, say, is in part the judgement that this is something bad, and the fear is in part the judgement that something bad will happen (such as the fear that the animal will tear you limb from limb). These passions are of course *more* than just judgements. The Stoics maintained that they were also quite literally movements of the soul, since they held that the soul is material and all its workings are to be explained in terms of its physical characteristics including movement; and passions are also impulses that cause actions.

The Stoic emphasis on the passions being judgements may seem counterintuitive. Is it not the case that passions are what happen *to us*, not within our control? (This was the view of the ancients: *pathê* is a cognate of *pathein*, what one suffers or what is done to one; see Annas 1992, 103.) Whereas making a judgement is something that the agent *does*, not at all the sort of thing that happens when someone is *overcome* by passion. The key to understanding both how and why, according to the Stoics, we should strive to be free of the passions, is to be found in appreciation of why they wanted to explain passion in terms of judgement.

How are passions connected to our experiences? Are they merely 'blind surges of affect, stirrings or sensations that are identified, and distinguished from one another, by their felt quality alone' (Nussbaum 1994, 369)? No: the passions have an essential cognitive component without which they would not be able to serve, as they do, as ways for us to relate to what goes on in the world. Passions are grounded in how we find the world, in how we judge matters; this being so, passions can be evaluated as appropriate or inappropriate, justified or unjustified. An evaluation that we have been slighted, for example, justifies and makes sense of our angry response. My feeling angry, and my displaying anger, only makes sense in a context where I believe (whether I really have reason to or not) that I have been treated unjustly, have been taken advantage of, insulted or something of the sort.

In response to any display of passion (or when we have some other reason to believe that an agent is in the grip of some passion) we may enquire of the agent the reason for the passion, and any satisfactory response will feature a reference to a set of beliefs about how the agent regards the world. With respect to our example of anger, not only must the agent believe that they have been slighted, or what have you, but they must also believe that this is *bad* for them. Someone may, for example, believe that their possessions have been stolen. They could not feel distress about this unless they also believed that the loss of the possessions constituted a harm, which was bad for them. Furthermore, the objects or events that concern us, and to which our passions attach, must be fairly substantial – that is, the way they matter to us must be fairly important, for as Nussbaum (1994, 370) points out, we don't live in fear of our coffee cup getting broken, we don't get angry at the theft of a paperclip, or pity someone who has lost a toothbrush.

On this view, we can maintain with the Stoics that passions can always be avoided by deciding to withhold our assent to the effect that anything really good or really bad is happening to us. If I do not judge that I have been slighted, I will not be angry. If I do not judge that I have suffered a loss, I will not be distressed at the destruction of my Ming vase. Certainly, I *could* do this, if I did truly believe that I had not been slighted, and if I did not think the loss of my Ming vase a true disaster. But surely these things do constitute genuine harm? And does not my winning a vast fortune in the lottery, for example – such that I can both solve my financial problems and live in luxury to the end of my days – constitute a genuine good? Most people would say so. But the Stoics say not.

This is because the Stoics maintain that only the virtues and virtuous acts are genuinely good, while only the vices and vicious acts are genuinely bad (see Long and Sedley 1987, §58, pp. 354–9). Other sorts of things usually held to be beneficial or harmful – or neither – are the 'indifferents'; these are such things as health, wealth, possessions, status, relationships, physical beauty, intelligence, sickness, poverty, lack of possessions, lack of status, few relationships, ugliness, dim-wittedness, etc. Some indifferents are preferred, some dispreferred, and some neither (such as whether someone has an odd or an even number of hairs on their head; Long and Sedley 1987, 58B2, p. 354). Stoics pursue preferred things, not because they are good, but because it is 'appropriate' for human beings, in virtue of the nature of the world and in virtue of the sort of creature that we are, to do so. (Thus, it is appropriate to prefer health, for instance.) What *results* from virtuous acts and from vicious acts is not respectively good or bad – but is preferred or dispreferred.

For the Stoics, then, *all* passion is inappropriate because having any passion can occur only in the circumstance that the agent has an attachment to something that can be only properly preferred or dispreferred. Failing to get or to preserve what is preferred cannot constitute a good, and getting or enduring what is dispreferred cannot constitute a harm.

If this view is correct, we are faced with a simple choice. Either we recognise the nature of the world and our own natures as rational creatures within it, in which case, if we *really* embrace the legitimacy of our perception, we would simply stop having passions, which among other ways of unpacking 'embracing this perception' would overall constitute a genuine spiritual transformation after which our rational natures are fully realised, or we ignore the Stoic perception and fail to realise our potential as rational creatures.

The Stoics say that we should take the Stoic path because this is the very best that we can achieve; the taking of any other path would be irrational. Does this not leave the follower of the Stoic path moving away from what most people would regard as truly human towards resembling a sort of machine, an unfeeling android from a science-fiction story?

Not altogether. The Stoic will be *apathês*, without passion (not apathetic, but dispassionate), but not wholly without feeling. It is impossible for the Stoic to eliminate purely physiological responses, such as starting at an unexpected or loud noise, or feeling faint in excessive heat (cf. Long and Sedley 1987, 65Y, p. 419) – as we all do, the Stoic will have the usual physiological response, jumping or keeling over, but they will also have the usual phenomenological feelings that accompany such responses. But the Stoic will, they claim, also have three 'affective responses', the 'good feelings' (*eupatheiai*): watchfulness (*eulabeia*), wishing (*boulêsis*), and joy (*chara*) (see Long and Sedley 1987, 65F, p. 412). Nussbaum (1994, 398) describes these as 'motivations that will help [the agent] steer her way among things indifferent'. Instead of being fearful, the Stoic will be watchful; instead of having desire, they will wish; and instead of feeling delight, they will feel joy (there is no 'good feeling' that correlates with distress, the fourth of the primary passions). These special feelings do not arise from judgements that good or bad things are happening or will happen but from purely rational considerations that the agent is exercising their capacities as well as possible in the appropriate pursuit of what is preferred. Judgements are still required. But instead of saying, 'I feel delight because I have obtained something good' (this judgement will always be false), the Stoic says, 'I feel joy because I have appropriately secured a preferred indifferent.' It is hard to see that the phenomenological content of the passion and the good feeling must always be different – indeed, we may decide that they must always be the same – but it seems coherent to hold that the first judgement has as its object a non-existent good, whereas the second judgement has as its object an existent indifferent.

The Stoics' case is sound. *If* it is the case both that the distinction between good-and-bad and preferred-and-dispreferred-indifferent things is legitimate, and if it is true that only my acting virtuously is good for me (or my acting viciously is bad for me), then it would be right for me to abandon the passions. If I ostensibly accept the truth of this, but do not immediately act dispassionately, this will reflect to what extent I have not properly embraced the Stoic theory of the passions rather than the extent to which the theory is mistaken.

If I wish to throw in my lot with the rational creatures of this universe, I must move towards embracing the Stoic theory of the passions. In practice, the more I moderate my emotional response to circumstances, the easier it is to see how inappropriate and irrational an emotional response would be, and the easier it is to see how the only good I can enjoy in this world is that good which I can secure for myself by striving to perfect my rational and virtuous natures, and become truly *apathês*.

The Stoics then offer us a stark choice. Either we carry on as we have been doing, abandoning ourselves to the lure and pull of 'externals', over which we have no control, held to ransom by feelings and emotions that the world at large stirs up in us, or we take a stand and recognise – if we can – that the Stoics were right to declare that our sole good lies exclusively in embracing a life of virtue.

How can we stop ourselves falling prey to the passions? We need to repeat to ourselves over and over again that anything 'good' we come across is merely a preferred indifferent. If we find a twenty-pound note in the street, if we get a rise, if we seem to be favoured in any way, we must say that this is not really something good for us; our various projects and interests may indeed be furthered by such eventualities, and it is rational to prefer a life that contains more, rather than less, incidents of this sort. Indeed, it is to be *preferred*, and should we be so blessed, we can make ours a *good* life only by *being good*, by acting well, by acting virtuously.

And when 'bad' things happen, we must say immediately that this is not really bad – for we have not (if it is true) acted viciously. All that has been harmed is my project, whatever it may be. In acting well I have done all I can do and all that is required to secure a good life.

This is such a strange way to view the world and the way we engage with it, that continuous effort must be made to maintain progress in the life of virtuous wisdom. The Stoics recommended a variety of practical 'exercises' by means of which we can 'make progress'. Some require self-observation. As the Stoic Epictetus said, the Stoic philosopher 'keeps watch over himself as over an enemy lying in ambush' (*Enchiridion* 48.3, trans. Higginson). Seneca recommended a daily review of our affairs; in connection with the passion of anger (though this is applicable generally) he said:

> All our senses ought to be trained to endurance. They are naturally long-suffering, if only the mind desists from weakening them. This should be summoned to give an account of itself every day. Sextius had this habit, and when the day was over and he had retired to his nightly rest, he would put these questions to his soul: 'What bad habit have you cured today? What fault have you resisted? In what respect are you better?' Anger will cease and become more controllable if it finds that it must appear before a judge every day. Can anything be more excellent than this practice of thoroughly sifting the whole day? And how delightful the sleep that follows this self-examination – how tranquil it is, how deep and untroubled, when the soul has either praised or admonished itself, and when this secret examiner and critic of self has given report of its own character! I avail myself of this privilege, and every day I plead my cause before the bar of self. When the light has been removed from sight, and my wife, long aware of my habit, has become silent, I scan the whole of my day and retrace all my deeds and words. I

conceal nothing from myself, I omit nothing. For why should I shrink from any of my mistakes, when I may commune thus with myself?

'See that you never do that again; I will pardon you this time. In that dispute, you spoke too offensively; after this don't have encounters with ignorant people; those who have never learned do not want to learn. You reproved that man more frankly than you ought, and consequently you have not so much mended him as offended him. In the future, consider not only the truth of what you say, but also whether the man to whom you are speaking can endure the truth. A good man accepts reproof gladly; the worse a man is the more bitterly he resents it.'

(Seneca, *On Anger* 3.36.1–4, trans. Basore 1928, 339–41)

One further exercise that Seneca alludes to throughout his writings is that of using our imaginations to anticipate disasters. When something 'bad' happens, of course we say that this is not really bad, but is simply dispreferred, but more than this, we can say that this is the sort of thing that can happen to creatures who are constituted as we are and who live as we do. It is nothing surprising, and it is not harmful, and we should not respond emotionally to it. We knew all along that it could happen.

But the new student who sets off in good faith with a view to practically testing this philosophy by honestly endeavouring to live it, must also be urged to read the Stoic writers as well as the secondary literature. For Stoic philosophy constitutes a *system* in which each part is connected to all the other parts, and it has not been possible to show how this works in this short paper. To orientate one's life as a Stoic, one will need to appreciate the Stoic views of the divine '*logos*', our relation to it and our participation in it, as well as the Stoic understanding of determinism, fate and providence. Many would say that this constitutes a mystical grasp of things, but striving to obtain it, the Stoics say, amounts to striving to perfect our rationality and our very selves. This, and possibly this alone, is what will mark us out as truly human.

SUPPLEMENT 1

SAMPLE RESPONSES TO STUDENTS' ASSIGNMENTS

Included in this section are my spontaneous responses to exercises submitted by actual students, lightly edited and revised (for the most part) in order to make them suitable for this new context. I hope that they will give to readers just a little of the flavour of what it would be like to participate in the course as a correspondence student. The topics included in the various sections below, and the treatment I make of them, were typical for a good proportion of students, so if you have written responses to the exercises at the end of the course papers, it is possible that some of the paragraphs below will give the illusion of my actually replying to you personally. Otherwise, I will hope that these additional attempts to elucidate Stoic ethics, and how to apply theory to practice, will help you make further progress along your spiritual path.

PAPER 1

Exercise 2

The main point, which I see you have grasped, is that it is not what we achieve by doing things that really counts, for the results are 'not in our power' and neither are the results likely to last very long (for even if they last a lifetime, they will eventually perish or be destroyed) – but what does count is the way we set about our tasks. How we do things is more important than what we gain, materially and practically, in doing those things.

Your dialogue is a very nicely written piece. You have homed in on several key Stoic ideas. Clearly, you have grasped the points that Seneca is trying to make. Although catastrophes of the sort Stilpo and Liberalis had to face are very rare, and of a sort that most people never experience, we all, nevertheless, face our own more private catastrophes, especially the loss of loved ones, the experience of debilitating or painful illness (in ourselves and in others), and sometimes financial problems, relationship problems, and other upsets. The Stoics teach that these things are facts of life, and that's that. And as you say, if we can change our core beliefs and attitudes, and come to see that the only thing of value is our good character, we can stand free from disturbance and cope with disasters on a purely practical level, as Stilpo did.

Few, I am sure, can ever attain this ideal, and the Stoics recognised this. But even if we fall short, by preparing ourselves for troubles, and rehearsing our responses to them, we will have achieved a great deal.

There is a further emphasis that I think it worth bearing in mind. The Stoics are keen to point out that the material goods we enjoy, including the people we come to know and have relationships with, are 'on loan from God', and that losing them is really no more than returning what we have been privileged to borrow (see Epictetus, *Handbook* 11). I have never deployed these Stoic principles to try to comfort anyone in emotional distress at the loss of something highly significant or at the loss of a loved one, and I doubt that such Stoic ideas would be at all well received. Such principles, I think, won't make sense to anyone unless they have a reasonably complete grounding in Stoic philosophy. Epictetus says that we should 'weep with' someone in distress (so long as we do not ourselves 'weep inwardly'; see *Handbook* 16), not that we should ply them with Stoic principles in an effort to get them to wake up to the truth of things!

PAPER 2

Exercise 2

We have power over our own intentions and judgements, but not over anything else. We can try to influence other things, and almost everything we do in life is indeed to try to affect other things, and other people. But to place all our hopes on success is foolish. It is best to do no more than wish, 'with reservation'. It is the way that we face affairs, and the way that we deal with both success and frustration that matters.

We need always to remember that when something is not in our power, it is 'nothing to us', as Epictetus says, because it is neither good nor bad. It is merely the material upon which we exercise our efforts in virtue.

Exercise 3a

In my view, being a philosopher in the way we are discussing means also having a certain sort of outlook generally, concerning what is truly important, and why, with the ultimate aim of living better and well. The philosopher, at least as much as the historian or the astronomer, for example, has the chance to develop a global or cosmic perspective, from which vantage point we see things from a very long view, and the short-term concerns of most people (not that no short-term concern can be important) seem ridiculous. For example, there is group of people building the Clock of the Long Now, which has a hand that will turn once in 10,000 years (about the same amount of time that has been covered by human history). They want to house the clock in a library that will contain all those things that are essential to human culture, both in terms of keeping a record of what that culture has done, and in terms of what it needs to survive if that culture should be interrupted (by a meteorite impact, for instance). Most people, I am sure, would not understand the significance of a clock that turns once in 10,000 years, or what it would mean to be (in 5000 year's time, say) the custodian of that clock. [See http://www.longnow.org/projects/clock/]

Exercise 3b

You have made a sound response. Personally, I think there is a problem for the philosopher who lives in society, yet does not share its values, indeed, thinks that they are positively harmful. For myself, I certainly feel that I am at odds with the world, even if I don't hate it (which I think I probably do, at least at times); and I certainly hope that I don't imitate it! (Well, not beyond driving a car to transport my disabled wife, and having an email account...)

Exercise 3c

I suppose seekers-after-gold-roofs want to be admired and liked by family and friends, as most people do. But Seneca's point, and also the general point of all the philosophical schools of the era, is that gold-roof-seekers have made a mistake regarding what someone should be valued for. If a Stoic had enough wealth to enjoy a gold roof, they would probably spend it on some community project or philanthropic cause. Gold-roof-seekers run the risk of inciting envy and social strife, whereas supporters of the community promote the brotherhood of humanity that the Stoics value.

There is also the objective of not being so frequently troubled by things. I think Seneca is quite keen to see a link between simple living and the serenity that the philosopher is trying to secure.

Entanglement with the material world is a distraction and possibly a threat to the philosopher, as dealing with material things and everyday affairs takes one's focus off the real issue of attaining virtue – until, that is, one has the knack of always responding to affairs appropriately even when they concern the things that previously would have posed dangerous distractions.

You are quite right – Seneca has always been open to and has been actively accused of hypocrisy, since for most of his life he lived in extreme opulence. His defence would be that for a Stoic trying to make progress, frugality is not essential, and that such opulence need not curtail one's progress so long as (just as you say) one can stay focused on one's primary task of living the virtuous life.

I think we need to see Seneca as being under the influence of forces he did not control. All that wealth was his only to the extent that the Emperor did not take it all away, which he could have done at any time on the merest of whims. Stoics always consider their property to be 'on loan' from God, as goods that are not really theirs. So Seneca has something of a defence against the charge of hypocrisy, and for us today, our real concern ought to be with the question as to whether Seneca's writings can help us in our own development. Our own progress as Stoics is not furthered by indicting and prosecuting Seneca.

PAPER 3

Exercise 2

You have asked me to comment on a specific text in Marcus Aurelius' *Meditations*, where he says:

> It is just as if the eye sought compensation for seeing, or the feet for walking. For as these were made to perform a particular function, and by performing it according to their own constitution, gain in full what is due to them, so likewise, *man is formed by nature to benefit others*...
> (Marcus Aurelius, *Meditations* 9.42 [last paragraph], trans. Hard, your italics)

Being of service to others (or to the entire Roman Empire, in Marcus' case) is an important theme in the *Meditations*.

Marcus Aurelius can be understood to be alluding to the 'Discipline of Action' (one of Epictetus' three 'disciplines' – of Desire, Action, and Assent; see especially Hadot's *Inner Citadel* for a complete account of this). The first discipline concerns what someone striving for excellence as a rational being should truly believe is worthy of desire, and this, for the Stoics (as we have seen) is that which is truly good, comprising only virtue and action motivated by virtue. The second discipline concerns our 'impulses to act and not to act' (as Epictetus puts it at *Discourses* 3.2.1–6), that is, our intentions and motivations, and directs us to what we each should aim for as an individual in our own unique set of circumstances to successfully fulfil the role of a rational, sociable being who is striving for excellence. The Discipline of Assent concerns using our impressions properly, such that we do not assent to false impressions (in particular, to the impression that anything is good or bad, when really it is indifferent) when making the transition from simply having the impression *of* something or other, to a declaration *that* what we are experiencing is either good or bad, really advantageous or really disadvantageous (see Epictetus, *Discourses* 1.4.11, 1.21.1–2, 2.8.29, 2.24.19, 3.12.8–15, 4.6.26).

The basic Stoic injunction, as we have seen in this paper, is to 'live in accordance with nature', and it seems clear what is required to satisfy this when we consider communal living. It means participating and contributing in fitting ways. In our modern, urban way of life, many people are inclined to view their wider community as a resource to plunder and exploit for their own selfish ends. And those who are exploited (by far the majority, though they usually don't see it), well, they try to get by as well as they can, though more often as not they also have the mentality that all that matters is satisfying their own personal desires. And it seems to me that this outlook is required on the part of almost everyone for our modern economy to function in the way that those with real power wish it to function...

From the Stoic point of view, this is objectionable, because it makes it harder for people to understand the importance of the Stoic ethical outlook, in which what matters is the condition of one's inner self, and not one's possessions or status or power. From the Stoic practitioner's point of view it doesn't really make any difference to their own practice, except that one's endeavours will almost of necessity, it seems, take place against a background of ignorance and hostility (which is why Epictetus says specifically that the Stoic practitioner should not discuss their principles with 'uneducated' people; see *Handbook* 46). Which is not to say that people on other paths – religious paths especially – do not face the same difficulties in this regard.

But to get back to your query, just as eyes and feet have particular functions for the body to which they belong, Marcus conceives of the individual person having specific functions with respect to their family, friends, and the wider community. Whatever we are, parents, sons, teachers, students, and so forth, we will have specific duties with respect to those roles (most people will have more than one role, of course) – and the Stoic practitioner strives to fulfil those roles virtuously, that is, 'excellently'. It is usually fairly obvious what is required for any one role. The student, for example, should attend classes and not be late; they should listen to their teacher, do the reading, allow enough time for writing papers and get those papers in on time. Sometimes a student will help their teacher in other ways – I remember once I helped one of my teachers get their car going. This comes down to doing what is required to the best of one's abilities. If we do not attempt to fulfil the requirements of our roles to the best of our abilities, we may wonder whether anything of real value can be gained from being a student, parent, etc.

Epictetus especially talks about being in service to God – for it is, ultimately, God who determines which roles we will assume (see *Handbook* 17). It is our task to accept this service and do what is required in good spirits, despite frustrations and setbacks (which for the accomplished Stoic are not even regarded as such), just as the foot should accept getting muddy, because this is what often befalls the lot of feet, and if only it could do so, the foot would embrace its muddy existence if only it could see its role in this wider perspective. This wider perspective, this 'cosmic perspective', is something that Marcus is keen to understand and cultivate.

You replied to these points, saying: 'From your reply, I assume that something which Marcus does *not* mean is that man is naturally altruistic.' In one sense yes, and in another sense no. Marcus thinks that people are altruistic in an innate sense – the interest to co-operate within communities and to contribute in meaningful ways to their flourishing is innately part of what human flourishing is. The individual cannot flourish without contributing to the flourishing of the wider community. Even the hermit who lives alone is unlikely *never* to have contact with other people, and however minimal that contact may be, he will in all likelihood contribute, for example, to some people's spiritual inspiration and aspiration.

But clearly many people do not display any profound tendency to altruistic commitments, except within small family groups, and even here such an outlook is more likely found (is it not?) in mothers, rather than in other members of the family (as a general rule, I mean). There is a streak running through Stoic thought that surfaces in a few texts suggesting that people's natural tendencies to altruism is stifled, as they grow from children into adults, by the prevailing values in their society. It is thus not too difficult for someone like me to conclude that many of the values found in society today are contrary to the health of human individuals and to that of wider communities. And there seems little doubt that it is unhealthy for other species and the planet as a whole.

For most of human history, people lived in small hunter-gatherer groups, and indeed, in some parts of the world, a small proportion of people still live like this. It is pretty obvious that such groups could not survive without an innate altruistic outlook on the part of each individual in the group. Modern conceptions of ownership, status and power, and viewing others as well as the environment as resources to exploit for essentially selfish ends are very much as odds with the values and outlooks that were essential to the survival of the human species throughout its history.

My personal view is that this has got to change, drastically and soon, otherwise we will all be in a very sorry way. I see Stoic ethics as a worthwhile contribution to such change.

Exercise 3a

I think Seneca's point is probably quite simple. In order to live well and be good people, we do not need gold and marble, and that cheaper and simpler materials will serve just as well. After all, what are the gold and marble for? To hold up a roof. What for? So as to use a room. What for? For entertaining my friends (say). So what really matters? Being a good friend, or having gold and marble to sit them under?

Yours is a very sound analysis, and I think you grasp all the points that Seneca wants to make. But, over and above our being free from the envy of others, and from the risk of having our thatch stolen, I think Seneca would want to say that simplicity in one area (having a basic dwelling, say) automatically leads to simplicity (and less trouble generally) in other areas. This is certainly an idealised view, but there is undeniably some degree of truth in it. In a fairly obvious way, the more you do, the more you get entangled in affairs; the more ambition you have and the more wealth you strive for, the more trouble you procure for yourself.

The key thought here is perhaps that, in living the more simple life, we will find it easier to live the philosophical life. Being attached to fewer concerns and having fewer distractions, we will be able to focus better on 'living according to nature'.

The idea of slavery is intended as a metaphor or simile – one can become enslaved to one's possessions like someone enslaved to another person, forced to do their every bidding no matter how undignified this may sometimes be, and no matter how contrary to your preferences and real interests. Seneca must have known people for whom this simile was horribly accurate – and perhaps many people are prone to it in all cultures and at all times – people who get up and carry on their activities for the benefit, so to speak, of their possessions. It is best that our possessions serve us and our interests, and obviously affairs have gone wholly awry when someone ends up serving their possessions.

Seneca's overall point seems to be that the problems people experience can often be put down to their desire for material goods of one sort or another. Though I think Seneca would agree that it is not fair or productive to blame and criticise individuals for their outlook, since it is society at large that sets the standards by which people are accorded status and value – and, alas, most people today, no less than they did in Seneca's time, seek to prove themselves in terms of acquiring wealth and material goods.

Yes, I think you are right, the Stoic will be happy to emphasise this point about the philosopher (the Stoic philosopher, that is) being less disturbed by emotional turmoil. But I wonder whether this goes deeper still. The reason as to why the philosopher is less troubled by the emotions is because they have learned to value things in a completely different way from other people, and this, surely, counts as a deep and unbridgeable gulf between the philosopher and the non-philosopher. It's not just that the philosopher will not get annoyed when their SUV gets scratched maliciously – the philosopher will probably not have and not want an SUV in the first place. If the philosopher acquires a huge great car, that will be because they can fulfil their obligations to others in no other way: and such a scenario is conceivable. Or put another way, the philosopher's desire was to be a good parent or friend, or what have you, and not for the car. The car was a means to an end. For the non-philosopher, probably the car was desired for its own sake, or if it was desired as the means to an end, that end would be something like wanting to impress other people. The car was not desired as a car, but as a status symbol, and of course, the philosopher's whole endeavour has been to dispense with that sort of thing. The car example can be extended to other cases. This general idea can be viewed through the question as to why people get up in the morning, what motivates them, and why they want to do what they do. Answers to these questions are going to look very different when answered by the philosopher.

Exercise 3b

I think you are quite right! I suspect that people have changed very little since Seneca's time. As you know, the Stoics say that you do not flourish simply by owning more and more, and Seneca seems to be saying here that in focusing one's attention on acquiring more and more goods one will neglect those things that truly promote flourishing. Indeed, as you say, people have come to make the mistake that human flourishing is identical with (or nearly so) with acquiring possessions. There is a real danger that we can end up getting up in the morning and going through our daily routine purely in order to service our goods – instead of our owning our possessions, we are in danger that they will begin to own us!

I suspect there is a very real problem with people simply not knowing what the goal of life is – not that everyone gives the same answers, and some answers would be more than agreeable to a Stoic because they accord with the notion of 'living according to nature', as would be the case when someone says that they live for their family, say. But it is rather worrying that so many people do seem to think that what truly matters is owning possessions and pursuing pleasures.

I have the impression that quite often when people criticise the 'anti-materialist' or 'anti-technology' point of view, they maintain that it is plain silly and unrealistic (and probably something of a delusion) to 'get back to nature' and to live without the comforts and advantages that technology has produced. Of course, there are no doubt some people who do advocate living like our Iron Age ancestors! But I don't think Seneca, or most Stoics, would wish to hold such an extreme position. The problem is that too many people are slaves to the technology, as well as to the materialist ethos.

Exercise 3c

Your interesting point here is that the greedy person has made a mistake. The more they get, the more they want (though, we must imagine that some people do find that a specific greed for something can be satisfied, and so that particular greed would cease) – but our concern should be with the underlying mentality of greed, which sees certain goods as the end and purpose of living, which when considered from a more enlightened point of view are seen not to be. As I understand it, and hope to show in this course, one of the main objectives of Stoic teachers like Seneca and Epictetus is to encourage people to adopt this alternative perspective.

The real challenge, I suppose, is to get people to appreciate the point of asking such fundamental questions as 'What is really worth pursuing?', 'What are material goods for?' Perhaps if a multiple-choice selection were offered, most people would rank 'freedom from disturbing passions', 'peace of mind', 'contentment' fairly high up on the list. And if someone put 'huge wealth' at the top, we can ask, 'So what would huge wealth do for you?' and I think we can expect an answer like 'Well, then I wouldn't be worried about anything.' 'Ah, so it is peace of mind you really seek?'

Most people don't think about things in this way at all, and most people assume without thinking that the norms we find in society at large (suggesting that material goods have a high value) are right.

PAPER 4

Exercise 1a

Ah, but the matter we are aware of and experience with our senses is matter-blended-with-God. Matter in itself, conceived of as passive undifferentiated 'stuff', does not exist, since what exists must be something-or-other. So when you hold something in your hands, you are of course holding matter (just as modern science understands this), but this is not unformed, undifferentiated matter in its raw state. (Think of a tub of papier mâché before it has been made into anything. This is rather like undifferentiated matter. But to become something, it must be given form and characteristics of some sort.) Of course, we cannot directly experience matter in this undifferentiated state, as everything we experience must be a something-or-other, and have some sort of form. So this 'primary' sort of matter is an abstract idea.

The Stoic understanding of matter and God is quite a complicated one. Each is conceived of as a distinct type of matter, though neither can exist apart from the other. So, for any physical object, it is made of a blending of these two types of matter. The God-type matter is understood to be active, and it makes the object what it is: it stops a rock being just a pile of dust, and it makes a tree into a tree and not a pool of jelly (for example). I feel there is a connection here to the modern scientific understanding of what matter is and why it is how it is. The modern conception of atoms and molecules are analogous to the Stoic conception of passive matter, and the fields and forces that make atoms and molecules combine and form structures are like the Stoic conception of God. The one difference is that the Stoics thought of God as self-conscious and rationally intelligent, and I'm sure that (all?) scientists believe that the forces of nature are without such qualities.

Exercise 1b

Yes, you are basically right, but it is probably better to say that God, matter, fate, and cause and effect, are all aspects of the one reality. 'God' is perhaps best understood as the name for this reality. Matter identifies the stuff it is made of, fate is the overall pattern that this unfolding matter takes (in a temporal sense), and cause and effect is the manner in which this unfolding takes place.

God is, according to the Stoics, also a type of matter. Unlike the usual conception of God being supernatural, transcendent and separate from the physical world, for the Stoics God is actually a sort of 'stuff' that blends perfectly with the first sort of unformed matter; and when this blending has occurred, the world as we know it is the result. Which is why the Stoics are correctly and appropriately referred to as materialists: the only sort of 'stuff' they held to exist (admittedly, two sorts) is matter.

On this other point, I am inclined to think that you are mistaken. I believe that the view that 'if God is omniscient then we cannot be free' is wrong. Goodness, even people like us who are not God can experience (on a small scale) what God's omniscience is like. Just because we know what will happen (with a high degree of probability in our case, certainty for God) does not prevent this virtually certain event being the outcome of a free action (if it is). We may know a young child very well, and know that whenever she tries to throw bread to the ducks she always loses her balance and falls over. Our knowing this, and predicting it with virtual certainty, does not make any difference to the question as to whether the action of the bread-throwing was free or not. Similarly for God. If God knows everything, then some of his knowledge will concern our free actions.

I think we open ourselves to confusion by saying things like 'God knows everything in advance'. I think there is a mistake here. Now, I cannot claim any expertise in theology, but I don't think the theologians claim that God knows things in advance of their happening. As I understand this question, God does not know things at different times. We, who live in time, know things at certain dates, at certain moments of time. But we also know things in a 'dateless' sense. It is true that $2 \times 2 = 4$. But this is not true at any particular time, even though we discovered it to be true at some set date. All of God's knowledge is 'dateless'. If God knows ('datelessly') that on October 10, 2006 I write this sentence to you, then that, at that date is what happens. God will also know whether I do this freely, or whether I am under the control of an external force or agency (as would be the case were I to have been fitted with a remote control device so that a mad scientist can control the movements of my body – or even the contents of my thoughts – using his remote control device).

Exercise 1c

Yes. Fate is the entire history of the universe. It is the pattern that events form when they are spread out in time. The connections between events are causal. Nature, fate and God appear to be the same thing (the world as a whole) when viewed from different perspectives.

Whatever comes about is fate. The historical record detailing everything that has happened (not that any one person is ever in possession of this record in its entirety), is the structure that fate has (though, strictly speaking, we must also add to this all future events as well). Perhaps it is possible to think about this using a simile: if we let a jigsaw puzzle stand as a model for our four-dimensional universe, allowing for the different pieces to be the different events of history, then fate just is the way the puzzle fits together, or is, indeed, the whole puzzle. It is the body of the universe in its entirety. For the Stoics, fate and God are the same thing. Put simply, fate just is the history of the universe. It is the body of knowledge (possessed by God) that contains all the true statements about everything that happens (and contains no false statements). If this can be grasped, we can see that the notion of fate does not in the least undermine the reality of our free will. Some of the true statements in the complete body of knowledge known to God, I believe, describe our free actions. Fate does not make things happen. It simply is the fact of their happening. Richard Taylor has a good chapter on fate in his *Metaphysics* (see the Bibliography), and I address the topic in my own book on the metaphysics of time (Seddon 1987).

Exercise 2

Seneca's general point seems to be that it is rather silly, if not self-indulgent, to get upset at things whose likelihood, if not inevitable, has been know to us all along. This is what life is like... One obvious exercise that Seneca seems to be suggesting is the deliberate and conscious anticipation and rehearsal of what might happen. The thought here seems to be that the blow from something rehearsed will be easier to take, or at least easier to recover from. Even if we are still upset by setbacks and catastrophes, at least we will not be surprised – at least not in general terms.

This example, of loosing one's slaves, needs to be set against other sorts of disasters, and in comparison it is really not that bad. This exercise can be applied to anything undesirable happening. Most things that happen are not that far along the scale of undesirability. Appreciating this ought to make troubles that much more easy to bear.

What Seneca does not do here, but which we can find in other writings, is to explain how Stoic principles can, for those who sustain and make progress in their practice, eliminate all concern for the things that happen, no matter how 'terrible' they are usually taken to be. As we have seen, the core Stoic principle is that virtue is the only good, and vice the only evil. Once we truly accept this, that troubles concern only our interests and undertakings, but never ourselves, we make ourselves immune to anything that can happen. This is an ideal, but one to which some people appear to have made a very close approach.

Exercise 3

'Indifference' is not really the psychological attitude of the Stoic wise person. Things that are not good and bad (everything apart from the virtues, that is) are indeed 'indifferent' – but this means indifference with respect to being good or bad, and is not really meant to signify a mental state. The Stoic wise person is committed to acting wisely and fulfilling their duties according to their station in life, but they are not attached to either the outcomes of their actions or to external objects and people (i.e. 'indifferent' things).

This is quite a difficult and subtle point, because we are so used to the idea that commitment requires attachment and a passionate engaging in affairs. This is precisely what the Stoics deny. It is attachment, to people, things, and outcomes, which is the whole source of our troubles.

Exercise 4

It looks like the life of military service was a universal metaphor in the Stoic school (Epictetus uses it as well) – that the Stoic wise person is in service to God, that life is a mission assigned to one by God, one's commander. So, in life, striving for what we want as individuals confuses our mission to do what the commander/God wants. (Though there is much more to say about this, including the fact that God wants what is best and appropriate for everyone.)

But care is needed. The danger of the military and games analogies is that they give the impression that the Stoics think that life is a game or a battle. This is to take the analogies the wrong way. All analogies are partial, as it is only certain features we want to point to as being common between this setting and this other setting. The emphasis in the games analogy is on athletic training, where the training is likened to philosophical training. The training is for something – it is to prepare us for the realities of life (philosophical training) or the rigors of competing in the arena (athletic training). The analogy of military life focuses on service – service to one's country in military service, and service to God in the philosophic life. It also focuses on the variety of jobs that must be done for one's military unit to function. Just as the commander sets out our duties for the day or for the mission (whether or not we like those duties), so God has set out our duties in life. So in life, we are not competing for medals nor fighting an enemy, as these aspects of the analogies are not intended.

Exercise 5

You have made a good Stoic response. A lot of people today would find this outlook quite incomprehensible, I think, as most people unquestioningly accept that one should aim for a life of ease and pleasure (not altogether quite as Epicurus thought of it...). Though, it's odd how many people will put up with almost intolerable hardships to acquire the ease they want (such as working long hours, or taking hours to commute to work by car or on the train).

The essential point is perhaps that if we didn't have any hardships to face, we would not really have very much to do in life, and we wouldn't be able to develop 'character'. I have asked myself who I would rather spend an evening with, someone who has never had to face a single difficulty in the whole of their life, or someone who has faced many and varied difficulties.

A lot of people, not all of them non-Stoic in my experience, find Seneca's emphasis depressing and morbid. Perhaps it seems so more readily to those who have had life relatively easy, but to those who have experienced pains and hardships of one sort or another, this view must sometimes come as a blessed insight that goes some way to explaining what life is all about. Some would view the idea that there is purpose in suffering to be trite or cruel, and indeed, some instances go way beyond what can be accepted as reasonable and sensible for a beneficent and providential God. So the mystery of suffering, in my view, is not altogether solved by Stoic theology.

Anyway, you have made a very good analysis of this topic. Your final point is quite right, that the Stoic sage is immune to hardships, so therefore cannot experience them. Of course, this is the position that Stoic students aspire to attain, and seeing the enduring of hardships as training exercises in our development seems sensible, as it seems essential that we should experience hardships in order to be in a position where we can evaluate our experiences. Although immune to hardships, the Stoic sage will still evaluate them as dispreferred and harmful to their projects, and also dispreferred in the sense that some hardships cause physical pain (fire, extreme cold, illness, hunger, etc.) – the sage experiences the pain, but is not troubled by it. This ideal, though worthy of pursuit, is probably very rarely attained!

I cannot see any references in which Seneca actually advocates pursuing hardships, and his overall point seems to be that having a hardship fall upon one should be viewed as something to find advantage in. It does not follow that more suffering is better. What you say is a perfectly sensible response to Seneca's 'suffering is beneficial' theory. What Seneca's theory has going for it is perhaps the practical point of making the best of things. It is surely worse to be overwhelmed by one's suffering, and in such a state miss opportunities for noble living, and better to take it on trust that we will be better people for enduring and coping with adversity.

Maybe we won't cope; maybe we will suffer horribly, enduring mostly misery, missing all the opportunities (possibly few) for relief and lighter moments. But if we can put our suffering to some purpose, to be better friends to others who suffer, for instance, it seems to me that we have got for ourselves a better deal. This, I agree, is a pessimistic view of human existence, and I am not sure how well it can be argued for in the face of objections from someone who feels keenly that it is incorrect.

But I do like Seneca's remarks about being tested. I suppose the point is a fairly simple one – if we do not face (at least some) adversity, how do we know what sort of people we are?

And to be honest, in my experience, in a rough and ready way, as far as I can tell, people who have not experienced a reasonably swift and thick torrent of suffering (at least for a period of their lives) are the most dull and uninspiring people imaginable. I feel like saying to them, 'But you don't know what human life is really like – you've only lived half a life!' And it is from this group, I feel, that most unkindness and selfishness comes. But that is a very subjective perception...

Exercise 6

Thank you for your thoughts on God and suffering. If God can be seen as the cause of our suffering, the Stoic is keen to point out that God has also so constituted us that if only we can realise it, we have all that we need within us to become immune to suffering. In brief outline, the Stoic notion of suffering is that suffering results from assenting to false judgements (about oneself and one's true nature, and about the nature of the world and what happens in it); false judgements can be replaced by good ones, and one can train oneself to make it less likely that one will assent to false judgements in the future. The Stoics do not of course claim that there is no such thing as pain, that would be absurd, but they do claim that it is possible to face and prevail over mental pain, anguish and distress. No one's capacities are inexhaustible or wholly invulnerable, and, as you know, the Stoics also had a doctrine of suicide, to the effect that if one's life becomes too burdensome it is rational to take one's leave.

PAPER 5

Many thanks for your email in which you remark that you are currently proceeding through Paper 5 with some difficulty because, as you say, 'it is not easy to change one's perspective on society, formed over a lifetime.'

Yes, indeed. Stoic progress is a long-term business. It takes a great deal of effort and persistence to free ourselves from long-established habits. Our responses to people and events generally are pretty much automatic, and it can be quite disorientating to have to remind oneself in the course of daily life that on any one occasion this evaluation is mistaken, or that that response is inappropriate. One thought, at least at the outset, is to focus on maintaining the Stoic outlook for only a short space of time – whilst you do just one thing in particular. And whilst doing this, two main features need to be held in your conscious mind: that (1) all actions are undertaken with reservation (the action will succeed unless something intervenes), and that (2) if something does go wrong, this is not anything bad, because one's primary aim is to maintain one's inner disposition in the right condition. Something going wrong with respect to one's undertakings cannot make a good disposition into a bad one, not unless we make the error of assenting to a false impression, and judge that something is bad when, as Stoics, we have already committed ourselves to the understanding that it is neither good nor bad, that it is indifferent, and that our peace of mind is completely independent of what has just happened.

Exercise 1

Yes indeed. Other people are responsible for what they do, and if what they do is shameful, well that is their own affair – subject to those circumstances in which we have reason to think we have a responsibility to mend someone's ways. When we come to thinking about how we ought ideally to interact with other people, we must remember that our capacity to influence them may not be zero (we won't know until we try), and it may sometimes be appropriate to try to influence people (for a whole variety of reasons). But we are responsible not for having the desired result, but only for trying wisely. And if we do not get the desired result – our trying was exercised 'with reservation', of course – we will not be troubled.

However obscure they are, there will be reasons as to why people are not as considerate as we would like them to be. But as Stoics, we can use those situations in which we have to deal with people to practise the virtues. The more we practise, the more that troubling situations will seem less and less troubling.

Exercise 2

The Stoic response to anyone's feeling anxious about what other people think of them seems to be essentially very simple. That is, your own conduct is in your own power, and this is the only thing that you should be concerned about. If other people judge you, whether to praise or criticise, that is their affair. So long as we do our Stoic duty with respect to others, treating them in ways that are right and proper for the roles we have, we can do no more.

Our responsibility is primarily to ourselves, to find and live by morally defensible guidelines (which will have to include how we deal with other people), and if we can make progress in this (not necessarily as Stoics, but for some people as Christians, or Buddhists, and so forth) it doesn't matter what other people think, except perhaps on those occasions when we have reason to think we are in the presence of an accomplished spiritual guide, and then we will listen and learn. But otherwise, we should be deaf to what other people think; for every person who approves of us, there will be someone else who does not.

The idea that the Stoic should promote justice (or any virtue) in others is hard to come by in the literature. I suppose this is because the Stoic writers always suppose that they are merely making progress, so should not condemn others from a position that falls short of perfection. Still, some wrongdoing is plain enough to see, and with care I am sure it is possible to react to it in ways that improve the situation rather than make it worse, and encourage greater virtue in the wrongdoer. Though, there is a general tone in the literature along the lines that almost all uneducated people (uneducated in Stoic ethics, that is) are beyond hope and help, and that the duty of the Stoic is always to attend to their own responses to wrongdoing rather than weigh in and try to correct others.

Marcus compares himself to the ram who has the responsibility of protecting his flock, and dealing with wrongdoers effectively must be construed as one aspect of this role. We all preside over one type of social interaction or another, at work, at school, in the office, or somewhere. And wherever possible, the Stoic has the responsibility to promote smooth and effective social interaction.

So when you are insulted at work in the ways you have recounted, remember that this cannot be a harm to you directly, though it may well undermine the effective running of the office or the smooth interaction of the personnel. It is your project of being a good manager that is harmed, and it makes sense to respond to it in that light.

Exercise 3

This is a very good assessment, with which I agree. In one way Marcus, and all Stoics, do expect high standards of everyone, for this is what everyone is capable of if only they knew it. Indeed, to achieve such high standards is to acknowledge and express our humanity to the highest degree. But as we have seen, Marcus is realistic in accepting that many people just cannot attain this ideal, of which almost all of them remain ignorant. This being so renders to each and every Stoic the duty to teach others wherever possible. And this, somewhat disturbingly, especially in our own era of political correctness, results in the Stoic setting themselves up as better than others. In terms of Stoic theory this is how things are. But even Marcus, who as emperor enjoyed absolute power, seems to exemplify a strong humility, for along with moral superiority comes a deep commitment to the human race as a whole. On this view, any rational and self-conscious creature is responsible for all other creatures (including themselves), and (we now recognise) also for the environment at large. So the 'superiority' of the Stoic is not something put on like a suit of clothes to impress others. In many ways it is a burden, and often it is not displayed at all, but will be visible to those who care to look for it.

Exercise 4a

You have written a sound and complete analysis. Excellent. Seneca seems quite keen on the idea that the Stoic is best off when circumstances test their strength of character, so a friend in need is just the thing (Letter 9, p. 49 of Campbell). His interest in having a friend is not so that he has someone he can call upon in times of need, but that he may be called on when his friend is in need. This strikes me as being at the centre of the Stoic notion of the brotherhood of man. The brotherhood can flourish only when each looks out for everyone else, and one contributes to it by looking out for others, knowing that when you yourself are in need you will be supported (but your preference to receive aid from others is not the reason why you give it to them; there should be no tendency to think in terms of trade or quid pro quo). The

Stoic supports others because it is to their own direct advantage to live virtuously.

Seneca's view is that it is better to have friends than not have them, and this makes sense, as we can view the having of friends as a preferred indifferent. But if we do not have friends, that does not really matter, as whatever situation we face will be the material that we use to live the virtuous life.

Exercise 4b

This is a good way of putting it. The Stoics often talk of friendship as a type of service, which is how they think of all our dealings in society. Whatever we do, we ought to construe it as service of one type or another. The best life for a rational and self-conscious creature is one that provides service for other rational and self-conscious creatures (and also, I think, provides stewardship over other creatures that lack rationality and self-consciousness).

Your remarks are very interesting. Certainly, the successful Stoic student progressively abandons the spontaneously emotional reactions that most people experience in the course of maintaining friendships. It becomes progressively harder to be effusively enthusiastic or gloomily pessimistic about preferred and dispreferred indifferents gained or lost on the part of friends. For instance, I have found myself tempering the over-reactions of friends and encouraging a more objective and long-term view, and this seems to be valued. Not so long ago a friend of mine had some trouble that I don't fully understand, and they became quite hostile and uncooperative with me. I'm sure many non-Stoics would have broken off the relationship pretty quickly – I must say, it tested me to breaking point. But I saw my role as that of being a good friend who is able to offer any sort of support my friend needed. It is my part to be a good friend, not to expect them to be a good friend in return.

Exercise 5

I think it makes sense to strive for a reasonable balance between your own needs (to make a good profit on your enterprise) and the needs of the starving Rhodians. In taking a responsible attitude towards others, we must not neglect our own needs that have every right to be included in our deliberations. (There is a popular and rather silly misunderstanding as to what moral behaviour amounts to, that moral actions are those that benefit others at the expense of the agent themselves!)

In both these cases, of selling the corn and selling the house, the major point seems to be to what extent it is acceptable to deceive people. Just because they get what they want (if they have enough money to buy the house, or if they can afford the high price of the grain, that is) does not mean that, if they knew the facts, they would be happy about how they got what they did indeed want. But in the case of the grain, your reputation as a fair merchant would be at an end! You certainly have a motive to maximise your profit – that's what merchants do – but not always to the maximum degree possible, and probably never by deceiving people. If you don't tell them about the other ships, the people think they are in a different situation from the one they are really in, and that is deceitful.

I think you are right – the general Stoic outlook, as we discussed above, honours the notion that the wise person is a member of the brotherhood of humanity, and that in many ways in the course of daily life we will be able to exercise our 'duty of care' to other people. For the Stoic, honourable conduct is supremely more important than pursuit of short-term profit. One way to think of this problem is to imagine that you have temporarily been removed from the situation (such as being transported aboard the starship Enterprise) and you cannot remember who you were (maybe through the affect of a drug). You are informed that you are either the merchant, or a prospective customer. Now, you have no choice but to work out what to do, and what you would most like to happen, from a completely objective point of view.

Most certainly it would be wrong to be deceptive by telling outright lies. But what you appear to be proposing amounts to not disclosing all the facts relevant to the transaction. And I feel that the retort 'Well, if the purchaser does not ask specifically for more information, why is the vendor obliged to disclose it?' rests on the underlying acceptance that relations in the capitalist market system are essentially exploitative: the manufacturer obtains the maximum output from their workforce for minimum wages, and they sell to their customer at the highest price the market can bear – all intended to leave the manufacturer with the maximum personal wealth, the worker with the minimum personal wealth, and the customer with less personal wealth (though with their newly purchased goods, to be sure, but possibly not up to the standard desired, and almost certainly obtainable at a cheaper price elsewhere).

Diogenes is perhaps plain wrong: if the cost to us is low or modest, maybe we are obliged to tell others what would be useful for them to know. And I wonder if the difficulty here is not to be pinned on fundamental incompatibilities between capitalist practices and the Stoic ideal of brotherhood. As I have remarked, capitalist practices seem to work against that ideal (all, or some of the time).

The difference between the Stoic merchant and most non-Stoic ones (excepting the Buddhist merchant, and perhaps a few others) is that the Stoic merchant does not see engaging in the market as an opportunity to exploit people. Just as they would wish for others to be fair and honest, they themselves know that they are blessed with the capacity to actually be fair and honest. So long as their trade gives them a living, and that they have opportunities to exercise the virtues and to grow in spirit, they will wish for nothing more.

Exercise 6

Yes indeed. The Stoic will want to live virtuously, and this includes being just, which is to say that people should be dealt with fairly. Obviously, what counts as fair may not always be clear or certain. But in the case of attempting to sell an unsanitary house, it is pretty clear that in not telling the potential buyer that there is a problem with the house, one would not be treating them fairly. Even in the situation where we think the buyer should be more astute and pretty much expects to be deceived, their having this outlook or not does not alter the fact that the seller is in fact being deceptive. And that would not be acceptable practice for a Stoic who would also counsel against such behaviour being adopted by others, because (1) doing something immoral is a genuine evil (for the agent) and (2) treating people unfairly is 'contrary to nature'. I side with Antipater! If I went to buy a house, I would want the vendor to be honest with me!

It's funny how many people do not agree with this point of view (which is worrying). I am inclined to think that overall, Stoic philosophy aims to encourage people to behave decently. Not revealing the bad features of the house most certainly seems to be a failure to act justly. It is honourable to treat people justly, and I think it makes sense to be aware of how we would prefer to be treated ourselves if we were buying rather than selling a property.

There is one problem that I think I have noticed, and this is that people expect you to be lying and deceiving (to some extent). If you were to say to the buyer 'Well, I'll take only €100,000 to make allowance for the structural problem at the back,' they would immediately be suspicious that there must be a lot else wrong with it besides! Alas, we seem to be living in a society where openness and honesty are seen as weaknesses, so any open and honest action becomes immediately suspected of being a cover for some diabolical dishonesty.

I hope that in thinking about these examples you will see the value of what I take to be the Stoic position. Personally, I am inclined to propose that a Stoic wishing to respect their capacity for virtue would sell the house at a price that fairly represents the state it is in. Regardless of the purchaser's competence to judge the condition of the house or ask pertinent questions, my obligation is to treat them as I would a close friend or a family member. Otherwise, I undermine the brotherhood that I should be promoting. The Stoic vendor knows that if they are not asked the right questions they must not use the opportunity to sell at an unrealistically high price. If both buyer and seller were taken behind the veil of ignorance and deprived of all knowledge regarding which role they had, both would want the vendor to be honest, and both would want the buyer to ask pertinent questions. But in the absence of, or inability to put, those questions, they would still want the vendor to be honest.

PAPER 6

Exercise 1a

I'm pleased to see that the Stoic approach to death makes sense to you and suggests ways of coping.

The Stoic presumably responds that fear of one's end, in pain and with loss of dignity (which may, in fact, not actually happen to you anyway), should be met with courage, just as all other fearful situations should be met. Pain, and other dispreferred indifferents, can strike at any time, and need not necessarily have anything to do with death or illness. The pain and distress of such situations is just what it is, regardless of whether one goes on living or not.

How best to bear the loss of loved ones and close friends is a very difficult question. But in crude outline, the Stoic will say that this specific difficulty should be met in exactly the same way as all others, with courage, and with an understanding that everyone (and everything) must eventually be 'taken back' by God. The ending of individuals, people and things, is the means by which new things come to be, and the means by which we ourselves came to be.

Something that I deliberately avoided on this course was the question of suicide. You will have found it discussed in the texts, I am sure. If we cannot bear what is happening, and we do not over-dramatise something of small importance, the Stoic says that suicide is an acceptable course of action. One cannot even aim at virtuous activity if one's faculties decline beyond a certain point; so if all is hopeless, and one values being able to live with dignity, which sounds appropriate for a Stoic, 'leaving the smoky room' appears to be an answer, if not the only one. Another answer may be to accept that our faculties are vulnerable, and if they fade and decline, well that is how it is.

The questions of the meaning of life, of futility, and how we should face an essentially irrational world, are important and perennial. The difficulty with the 'futility' thesis, which essentially laments impermanence and lack of objective meaning in the universe, is one of getting clear on what a happy solution would look like. For people to live a very long time, and for their works to endure for centuries or millennia rather than just years or decades, does not really provide a solution. And what would count as 'objective meaning' for the person who laments its lack? A voice from the sky, claiming to be that of God, telling you how to live and what to value, might be believed and accepted by some, certainly; though that voice, already available in scriptures around the world, attracts only some people, and only a proportion of that number appears to have any real insight into its meaning. This is because meaning must come from within. The voice of God is of no use to us unless we understand from within ourselves what it is saying, and accept what it says.

The Stoics, of course, say that the apparent irrationality of the world is an illusion. This is the way things seem when we have not made the attempt to understand what is of true value and to adopt the 'cosmic perspective' that Marcus Aurelius is so keen on. From a wider objective viewpoint, the world is in fact rational, with everything ordered just as it needs to be for the whole history of the world to be just as it is (which is also just as God intends it). In resisting this perspective and sticking to a subjective point of view, of course we complain that the world is not being run for our own benefit (because we object to our plans being thwarted, to ill health and other misfortunes, and especially to how we feel about these things). But the Stoic, in not expecting the world to operate for their own benefit – at least not directly – but in understanding that their role is to contribute to the world by accepting and working with what fate brings, becomes immune to the irrationality question.

Exercise 1b

Epictetus and other Stoics would not object to 'still wanting to hold on to the people I love', so long as that 'holding on' is done in the right way. Recognising that anyone can be taken at any moment, and being ready to accept that event without giving way to overwhelming grief, does not mean that we do not love the people we want to 'hold on to'.

The Stoic is never surprised by anything that happens, not because they knew beforehand that it would happen, but because they already knew that it was the sort of thing that could happen. And they already knew that they have the strength of character to deal with it, so whatever its nature, there can be no objection to its coming about.

Epictetus would say that wanting friends and relatives to live forever (or for them not to die before we do) is simply failing to accept what is in our power and what is not. But understanding what is in our power does not in itself mean that we can accept this situation with complete equanimity. Knowing that something is inevitable, or even that it has been decreed by God, does not seem to make any difference as to whether it is bearable.

This further step of wanting things to be just as they are is hard to take, and maybe a genuinely firm acceptance is a rare phenomenon. The Stoic requirement does seem both demanding and contradictory, for we are to care for people, yet not be disturbed by their suffering harm and eventual dying, and by our losing them.

I think the ancient Stoics would want us to understand, and to live by that understanding, that it is possible to be earnest about our preferences (such as not wanting others to suffer harm, not wanting them to die, and not wanting to suffer their loss) but not to be overwhelmed by emotion when those preferences are frustrated.

Exercise 2

It certainly seems to matter that life is transient from the point of view of completing certain projects. Completing things is very important to us in this culture, and for many people I am sure, death is seen as something almost intentionally cruel that prevents any number of important conclusions. Epictetus says in the *Handbook* that someone in old age (and therefore as a matter of fact someone who can rightly suppose that they are nearing the end of life) should not get deeply involved in things (see *Handbook* 7). Maybe it is possible to use the 'act with reservation' exercise on a larger scale? Ordinarily we might say something like, 'I will eat this icelolly so long as it does not fall off the stick.' But maybe we can also say things such as, 'I will see my grandchildren grow up so long as I don't die,' or 'I will enjoy the spring next year so long as I live that long.' I have the impression that many people promise themselves things merely because they are possible and likely, whilst failing to appreciate even that what is likely all the same sometimes does not happen.

I like the 'coming ashore' analogy for what living a life is really like (*Handbook* 7, again). It shows the folly of forming the wrong sort of attachments to things (and to people). Seeing ourselves as temporary custodians and stewards places a completely different emphasis on wealth and property (on other people, and our own bodies). And the question as to whether we are taken somewhere else when we step back aboard the ship misses the point of the metaphor. The Stoics teach that it is possible to engage with the world in agreeable ways without getting worked up by what happens.

Exercise 3

I have always thought that the inn example also alludes to the idea that nothing is really ours, and that we merely have the use of things for the time being. (The topic of the next question, I realise!) Personally, I have become acutely aware of this with respect to the house I am living in, that my wife and I inherited in 1995. It does not feel like mine! I just have the use of it until I die or cannot live here any more (I plan never to live anywhere else, so this sense of 'merely having the use of' cannot be put down to having plans to move to a different house at a later stage).

The stopover metaphor, I think, is intended to disabuse people of the belief that anything is truly theirs. If it is possible to regard life as but a temporary stopover, the notions of ownership and possession begin to look somewhat foolish and misplaced. Instead, it is better to view what we usually take to be 'ours' to be merely in our temporary stewardship. It is the care we devote to these things that matters, and not the things themselves.

Exercise 4

The metaphor is supposed to encourage us to the realisation that just as all the things we make use of in an inn are just on loan, so are all the things we use in real life. Everything we possess is actually just on loan, and must be passed on to the next sojourner.

Exercise 5a

Clearly, the Stoics thought of the virtues as goods, and vices as evils, on a completely different scale from that of indifferent things. Yet evidently, the indifferent things can also be valued, only not in the same way, for undeniably we prefer some and disprefer others for fairly obvious reasons. In some situations, the Stoic might, for example, prefer death to life (various examples will be found in the ancient writings), and if this is granted, then the 'preferability' of life must lie in something separate from life itself. (And so for all other preferred, indifferent things.)

As I have come to understand this, what determines the preferability of things is the degree to which they contribute to living in conformity to nature. In general, one conforms to nature by living, by maintaining good health, by taking care of one's relations and friends, and by looking after one's property. Further, one should also strive to adopt wise and coherent interests and projects, through which one may express one's rationality by committing oneself to various causes and ideals (even if they are simple and mundane).

The Stoic chooses virtue, and in a virtuous way, selects the preferred indifferents. But regardless of what we select and the outcomes of our projects, we are nevertheless wholly fulfilled, and perfectly happy. (Well, that is the ideal!)

I don't think the Stoics would object to your enjoying your indifferent external possessions. Enjoyment must feature somewhere, otherwise Epictetus' example of enjoying the festival of life will be a puzzle (*Discourses* 3.5.10, 4.1.104–5, 4.4.24). But as Stoics, our happiness does not rest in the things themselves, but in the way we use them, care for them, and share them with others. Our use of these things, as well our enjoyment of them, should be an expression of our honest efforts to live virtuously.

The Stoics do not mean to deny us an emotional life. They want us to relate to the world with feelings that express our virtues, and most definitely not to go so far that we fall prey to the 'passions' or 'violent feelings', which almost certainly will result in vice.

Exercise 5b

The understanding of what is in our power helps us change the focus of our attention to how we react to things and the judgements we make about things, rather than the things themselves (which lie in the province of fate, outside our complete control). It is the judgements that we make and the emotional reactions we have towards things that undermines our well-being. Getting clear on the notion of what is 'in our power' helps us get a better grip on how we evaluate things and respond to them.

Exercise 6

What you say is about right. But it's not that we pessimistically expect that things will go wrong or turn out badly, but that we recognise the possibility that they could. In short, if they do turn out badly we have no grounds for being surprised or for feeling frustrated. Indeed, whatever happens must be viewed as an opportunity to exercise our skills in virtuous action.

There is a fine line to walk when trying to act with reservation, because I think it might be easy for some people, and I include myself here, to begin to expect the worst over and above anticipating it. One can then easily set about things already quite convinced that something will intervene and prevent progress or success. (But there is still the advantage of not being surprised or upset when it all goes wrong!)

Exercise 7

The best text I can find that gets close to a 'nutshell' definition of nature and its role in Stoic ethics is this extract from Diogenes Laertius:

> Zeno was the first (in his treatise *On the Nature of Man*) to designate as the end 'life in agreement with nature' (or living agreeably to nature), which is the same as the virtuous life, virtue being the goal towards which nature guides us. ... Again, living virtuously is equivalent to living in accordance with experience of the actual course of nature, as Chrysippus says in the first book of his *De finibus*; for our individual natures are part of the nature of the whole universe. And this is why the end may be defined as life in accordance with nature, or, in other words, in accordance with our own human nature as well as that of the universe, a life in which we refrain from every action forbidden by the law common to all things, that is to say, the right reason which pervades all things, and is identical with this Zeus, lord and ruler of all that is. And this very thing constitutes the virtue of the happy man and the smooth current of life, when all actions promote the harmony of the spirit dwelling in the individual man with the will of him who orders the universe. Diogenes then expressively declares the end to be to act with good reason in the selection of what is natural. Archedemus says the end is to live in the performance of all befitting actions.
> (Diogenes Laertius, *Lives of Eminent Philosophers* 7.87–8 [with omission], trans. Hicks 1931, 195–7)

Once in a while I have encountered people who seem to have been under the misapprehension that when the Stoics justify their ethics appealing to nature, this must mean that if anything occurs in nature, then it is justified and proper for human beings to do it. That isn't it at all, I'm afraid... By 'natural', the Stoics mean 'proper to this particular creature'. It is natural for cows to eat grass, but not for fish or people to do so. It is natural for gibbons to swing through the treetops, but not for elephants or blue whales to do this. And so on.

Clearly, nature is a guide to what is proper for any particular creature. Certainly, aberrations occur (I think I have heard that sometimes individual chimpanzees can indulge in cannibalism, for instance), but it does not follow that any instance of any behaviour on the part of creature X is right and proper for all Xs at all times.

The ancients were interested in excellence and what makes any specimen an excellent example of its kind. It is from this notion of excellence that we get our concept of moral virtue, and we can use 'virtue' in phrases like 'in virtue of what is this a good example of an X?' Wherever possible, it seems that nature promotes excellence. Given the right resources, any specimen will grow into an excellent example of its kind. Of course, most individuals have their excellence compromised in one way or another, but this does not prevent us from working out what excellence consists in for the particular type of thing we are looking at. And this is no less true for ourselves, for human beings.

It is pretty obvious what is required for excellence in human beings. To live well and to thrive, a person must have adequate food and drink, must be protected from the environment with appropriate clothing and shelter, and, because human beings are social creatures, they should – to live well – live in communities where their members support all the other members according to their needs, skills and capacities.

Nature tells us directly and in obvious ways that certain sorts of actions are 'contrary to nature', such as poking out someone's eyes. Without your eyes, you cannot thrive, and possibly you cannot live at all. Such an eventuality would clearly be detrimental to those who have their eyes put out. But the person who commits such violence cannot be said to be living well themselves, or living according to nature, for now they are undermining their own community and the capacity of that community to thrive as nature intends.

If something is 'preferred', this is because nature has made us this way. We prefer to eat well, rather than poorly or not at all, and we cannot do this if only grass is on the menu (though a sheep would see this all quite differently). But we are undermining our community if we seek to eat well at the expense of others (by putting out their eyes so that we can steal their lunch, for example). And so on and so forth for other sorts of things. This is why the Stoic pursues what is preferred in a virtuous way, treating others justly, facing dangers with courage, and acting with self-restraint, choosing their activities and carrying them through wisely.

It is important to emphasise the role of rationality in the way the Stoics understood their maxim, 'Live according to nature'. One way to interpret the maxim is to rephrase it as 'Live according to the way we have been constituted by nature.' And this means 'live rationally'. The one thing which sets human beings apart from the rest of the animal kingdom is our capacity for reason. The reason why we have this capacity at all, say the Stoics, is that we each possess a small part of God's rationality. And what God intends is that we use this capacity properly and to its maximum potential. The way to do that is to live a life of virtue, which means exercising the virtues on a moment by moment basis.

As we have seen, Epictetus especially likens the mental discipline of exercising the virtues with exercising the body to build one's strength as an athlete. When called upon, we must be ready to face and deal with any eventually as fully rational and fully responsible self-conscious and rational beings. Our capacity to do this is a privilege we have, but it is also a duty we owe to God. The Stoic would say that whilst everyone pursues the preferred indifferents (though not necessarily doing so very well), only the Stoic Sage, who is fully virtuous, can do so properly. And of course, how we engage in this pursuit is more important than what we secure by engaging upon the pursuit.

Perhaps it would be best to say that the Stoic can be earnest and dedicated, enthusiastic and determined – yet they do not judge any setback as bad, nor any successes as truly good. What is good is their disposition, the equanimity they experience and which they bring to and maintain throughout each and every undertaking.

Exercise 8

There is also the point that valuing things in the wrong way can lead to all sorts of troubles. We can end up serving our possessions rather than having them serve us. Some people, I am sure, think their troubles will be over if they ever get to be rich. But once they are rich, then their troubles begin. The person who lives simply has been able to avoid or dispense with the encumbrances that inevitably attend upon dealing with affairs generally, and with caring for property and possessions. We live at a time, by no means unique, when many people seem to value their material possessions more than themselves. It seems quite plain that such people are convinced that happiness is rightly equated with the possession of property, and perhaps also with the exercise of power. They are mistaken, even if that is because they are misguided, and the folly they will bring down on the world as global warming runs on apace, whilst flights in passenger airliners increase, is obvious even to non-Stoics who care to think about it; it is no less obvious that our current system of values must be abandoned.

Exercise 9

Yes, indeed. And we can also review specific events to make sure that we applied the appropriate virtues well. If we went to the dentist, we should check to see whether we really were brave enough. Or if we faced a difficult person, we must make sure that we stayed calm and patient, and treated them well. If we failed, getting angry for instance, we can rehearse in our imaginations what we should have done, and resolve to do better next time.

And I suppose it makes sense to frequently remind ourselves that we are doing all this because we agree with the ancient Stoics – if we do – that this is what is appropriate for a rational, self-conscious being.

And there is also the aspect of appraising our past efforts to spot our faults and mistakes, and to try to work out why we made them so as to avoid similar errors in the future. Usually this amounts to constantly reminding ourselves of what is in our power, that indifferent things have only an instrumental value with respect to contributing to our projects which we should be committed to, but without being attached to.

Exercise 10

God is that self-conscious rational agency that organises matter to make the world we experience. But as fragments of God's rationality we directly participate in this process.

The Stoics were monists (holding that there is only one substance), and the soul they believed in was a material one. Material cannot be destroyed, it can only change in character, so in some sense everyone's soul must survive death of the body, though it is not at all clear to what extent the Stoics believed they would have any post-mortem experiences. This 'soul-stuff' pervades the whole cosmos, and is identified with God. So the little bit of it we refer to as 'our' soul, is understood to be a fragment of God, who is the soul of the universe. I see a level of consistency here with modern cosmological theory, exponents of which point to laws and principles that operate everywhere in the universe, and although the principles are not themselves material, they are manifest perpetually in the behaviour and characteristics of matter. It is these principles that structure and order the cosmos, not matter itself, and this, to me, looks very close to Stoic theory.

Exercise 11

In addition to what you say, I think there remains the possibility that it can be worthwhile, sometimes, taking steps to try to mend people's ways. This may mean on occasion pretty much pretending to be angry, to show them how unacceptable their behaviour is. The Stoic can adopt the usual social behaviour, but need not actually experience the emotion connected with it. The danger of calm acceptance (which is actually how we feel) is that we appear to be sanctioning bad behaviour. At other times, I think it can be possible to suggest new behaviour in a calm and considerate way, and actually get a worthwhile result precisely because we have not flown off the handle.

Yes. The Stoic does not get angry, because they do not believe they have suffered any harm, though their project might have been disrupted. It is not the success of any project that matters, but the conduct of the agent when working on the project. The person who causes the offence is the one who is harmed, because they are harmed just by the fact that they have indulged in vice and behaved viciously.

Exercise 12a

I suppose the Stoic idea of progress is in essence the progress away from fears, disappointments, frustrations and emotional disquiet of all sorts, to a thoroughgoing equanimity and contentedness with everything. The 'end', or goal, of Stoic ethics, is *eudaimonia*, which is usually translated as 'happiness', but which ought really to be construed in wider terms, and I think 'flourishing' is that bit better. Flourishing consists in more than just equanimity and serenity, though must include these items no matter what else it includes. And flourishing in this sense does not mean the success of all one's projects (indeed, all the Stoic's projects may fail whilst they themselves continue to flourish). Flourishing means to flourish as a human being, which must in part mean understanding fully what a human being is (what is in our power, how we should relate to God, the universe, the wider community, to family and friends, and to ourselves) and doing what a human being should do – which in outline is covered by the notion of acting virtuously at all times.

One of the earliest Stoic formulations of 'the end' is a 'smooth flow of life', which implies a number of things revolving around the notions of tranquillity and peace of mind (*apatheia*), and contentment (*ataraxia*). The emphasis seems to be that of being completely free from emotional disturbance. Later formulations of 'the end', such as 'living in agreement with nature' refer more to the techniques (living virtuously, for instance) by which a 'smooth flow of life' can be attained. If we define the end as that which we do for its own sake and not for the sake of anything else, a 'smooth flow of life' might seem a better candidate than living according to nature, because living according to nature can be construed as the means by which a 'smooth flow of life' can be secured.

Exercise 12b

I think a large part of the unhappiness that people feel is constituted by being overwhelmed by the emotions. Fully embracing and acting on Stoic teachings is likely to severely undermine this affect. A basic starting point that will be appreciated by most non-Stoics is to suggest that having one's preferences frustrated is bad enough, but that getting worked up about it only makes it worse.

Exercise 13

This is a strange metaphor, and I suppose the only way to interpret it is to suppose that we are in fact watching out for ourselves as if we were our own enemy. So what are we watching this 'enemy' *for*? We are watching for them to make a mistake, to react to something passionately, to behave viciously, to fail in some duty. But if possible, we need to catch ourselves just before we fail, so that we can correct ourselves. But either way we will correct ourselves, preferably before, but if not, then after the deed.

Until we get really good at it, maintaining a Stoic outlook is a fragile, and even an intermittent, thing. We need to watch ourselves in case we start to attach importance to things in the wrong way, in case we think something is good or bad, when it can be only preferred or dispreferred, and in case we react emotionally to something. In a way, we need to imagine ourselves always looking over our own shoulder saying things like, 'I don't think Socrates would have done it like this!' or 'I bet Epictetus wouldn't have said that,' or 'How would you feel about this if Marcus Aurelius were in the room watching you!?'

Even if we can't be Stoics all the time, I think that what these old texts do is suggest that we can think about things differently, and act as agents in a more rational and self-conscious way.

I sometimes wonder whether Epictetus was talking about acquiring a new and stronger self-consciousness. Human beings are not just conscious of the world, but they are conscious of being conscious. Yet, I find that when I try to 'watch myself' as I go about my affairs, I get engrossed in what I am doing and forget to watch myself in a matter of minutes. So I wonder whether Epictetus' point is that this 'watching ourselves', the accomplishment of which surely will result in fewer vicious actions, is something that we really do need to train ourselves in, in the most thorough of senses. I am left wondering whether the true Stoic Sage enjoys a fundamentally different type of consciousness.

The metaphor of watching ourselves also emphasises the earnestness with which this must be done, and also emphasises the danger we pose to ourselves as our own enemy. The only harm we can suffer is the harm that we do to ourselves.

Exercise 14

I'm pleased to hear that you have got practical benefit from the course.

I am inclined to agree with you about Seneca [that in his personal life he appears not to be a very good model of the Stoic Sage], and I debated for quite some time whether to use the *Discourses* and *Handbook* of Epictetus as the main texts. I decided in the end that Seneca is perhaps better for the complete novice, and Epictetus is better for those who are beginning to make progress. (Epictetus I feel is more effective for the student who already knows something about why he says what he says.)

Thank you for your exercises, which I have enjoyed reading. I am pleased to hear that the course has proved beneficial, and hopefully applying the Stoic outlook will be an advantage for you in the future.

SUPPLEMENT 2

KEY TO THE STOIC PHILOSOPHY OF EPICTETUS

The key to understanding Epictetus is found in understanding the notion expressed in Chapter 1 of *The Handbook* about 'what is in our power' or 'up to us' (depending upon which translation you use), though this notion cannot be properly understood without tying it in with other aspects of Stoic philosophy.

For Epictetus the key to the philosophical life is knowing what is really up to us, and this, he says, is maintaining our *prohairesis* (moral disposition or moral character – sometimes translated simply as 'will') in the proper condition. Within everyone's power are their impulses, desires and aversions – and exercising this power properly can be equated with the 'proper use of impressions'. The term 'impressions' for Epictetus refers to sense impressions of all sorts (but also to 'internal' or 'mental' impressions including memories, anticipations, conjectures, hopes and suchlike). When someone has an impression, such as having the taste of chocolate, immediately an evaluation of the impression is made – typically, that chocolate tastes good, and in this example the desire to eat more chocolate cake is the likely result. This is where our power really lies, in consciously stepping in so to speak to take charge of the connection between having an impression and making a judgement about it. If we make the wrong sort of judgement then the wrong sort of action is likely to result.

Opposed to the 'internal' things that are in our power are 'external' things that are not in our power, which include our health, wealth, status, possessions, and so forth. Epictetus says that we should try to manage these things as well as we can – we should strive to stay healthy, fix the roof when it leaks, do good works so as to maintain a good reputation, and so on. But these things are ultimately not ours to command. How others regard us, although influenced by what we do, is ultimately up to other people; whether we are ill or not usually depends upon factors we cannot control; and whether the roof stays on in a severe storm is down to forces over which we have absolutely no power at all.

Epictetus and the Stoics say that if we invest our well-being in these external things, we are doomed to disappointment and unhappiness. Instead, we should focus on our state of mind (on our *prohairesis*). If we make the right judgements about things, especially whether or not they are in our power, we have a chance to flourish to the best of our capacities.

What is good and bad, say the Stoics, is to be found in this 'inner' realm of what is in our power, and everything else (in the realm of 'externals') is 'indifferent' (that is, indifferent with respect to being good or bad). The Stoic finds no value in external things, so does not pursue riches or fame or power. The thing of most value to the Stoics and to Epictetus is having one's moral disposition in the right condition, and this is accomplished in most part by making the proper use of impressions (accomplished by judging the proper significance of things – essentially being aware of what is and what is not in our power).

The only morally good thing for Epictetus is virtuous activity, facing the world with wisdom and courage, living moderately and treating other people justly. One aspect of maintaining one's moral character in the right condition is having it engage only in virtuous activity (and never in activity motivated by vice). The Stoics often refer to this way of life as 'living in accordance with nature', which refers both to human nature and to universal nature. In living in accordance with human nature, the Stoic will engage in and promote co-operative and social living, understanding this to be what is 'appropriate' for human beings. To live in accordance with universal nature means accepting what fate brings us, and dealing with it as someone who has a moral character in the right condition. One aspect of living in accordance with nature is accepting that we are in service to Zeus (God), much as a soldier is in service to his commander. Living life, on this metaphor, is like being on a military mission, accepting the orders we are given, even if hardships must be endured, and even if we would prefer something else.

SUPPLEMENT 3

NOTES ON THE CONFLICT BETWEEN THE STOIC SCHOOL AND THE EPICUREAN SCHOOL

[Note: LS = Long and Sedley 1987.]

Epictetus criticises Epicurus and Epicureanism at several places in the *Discourses* (notably at 1.20.17–19, 1.23, 2.20, 3.7 and 3.24.37–9).

His main concern is that the Epicurean conception of 'the end' is mistaken. Epicurus says that the end is pleasure (and qualifies this quite extensively), and this directly conflicts with the Stoic notion of the end (identified as 'living in agreement', or 'living in agreement with nature'; see LS 21 and LS 61).

At LS 63A, Stobaeus says that 'The Stoics say that being happy is the end,' which identifies the end as *eudaimonia*, which is best translated as 'flourishing' rather than 'happiness'. But of course, Epicurus says just the same thing (see LS 21B2; at B1, 'happiness' translates *eudaimonia*)! The dispute concerns what constitutes *eudaimonia*.

The Stoics say that living virtuously is sufficient for happiness (LS 61A2, for instance), but Epicurus says that the virtues are merely a means to that end (LS 21P). So at the level of their most basic doctrines, the two schools disagree.

Another important concern for Epictetus is that over and above the Epicureans being in error, their teaching is also detrimental, both to society and to the individual (since, say the Stoics, pleasure is not sufficient for *eudaimonia* – indeed, it is not even constitutive of it – and failing to gain *eudaimonia* is an evil for the individual).

The Stoics hold that the capacity for virtue is innate (LS 61L, for instance), whereas Epicurus says that this is not the case (LS 22) and that 'not harming' is a social convention enforced by contract (22A). At 22B, Epicurus says that justice has a utility value, which is wholly at odds with the Stoic view. At 22H, he says that friendship should be pursued for the sake of the pleasure that can be gained by so doing. Epicurus is promoting a clear-cut egoism, whereas the Stoics teach a clear-cut altruism.

So in criticising the Epicureans, Epictetus is aware that he is trying to undermine the harm that he sees their doctrines as causing or promoting.

There are other differences as well. For instance, Epicurus teaches withdrawing from society literally, and leading the quiet life of retirement. The Stoics teach that one should take responsibility for one's community and contribute to communal life in a virtuous way; the Stoics hold that one may 'retire' from trouble and vexation without actually abandoning the attempt to contribute in a responsible manner.

The different views on God, fate and providence that the two schools adopt share absolutely nothing in common!

We must suppose that in Epictetus' time the opposition between the two schools was well known and vigorously contended. His students must have expected him to say at least something about what is wrong with the Epicureans, and it is perhaps surprising that not more of this conflict is portrayed in the *Discourses*.

BIBLIOGRAPHY

ANCIENT SOURCES

BASORE, J. W. 1928. *On Anger* (with others) [vol. 1 of Loeb Seneca, *Moral Essays*]. MA: Loeb Classical Library, Harvard University Press.

BONFORTE, JOHN. 1974. *Epictetus: A Dialogue in Common Sense.* New York: Philosophical Library.

CAMPBELL, ROBIN. 1969. *Seneca: Letters from a Stoic.* London: Penguin.

COOPER, JOHN M. AND J. F. PROCOPÉ. eds. 1995. *Seneca: Moral and Political Essays.* Cambridge: Cambridge University Press. [Contains *On Anger, On Mercy, On the Private Life,* and *On Favours.*]

COSTA, C. D. N. 1988. *Seneca: 17 Letters.* Warminster: Aris & Phillips.

———. 1997. *Seneca: Dialogues and Letters.* London: Penguin. [Contains three dialogues: *Consolation to Helvia, On Tranquility of Mind, On the Shortness of Life;* four of the *Moral Letters*: Letters 24, 57, 79 and 110; and three extracts from *Natural Questions.*]

DOBBIN, ROBERT. 1998. *Epictetus: Discourses Book 1, Translation and Commentary.* Oxford: Clarendon Press.

FARQUHARSON, A. S. L. 1992. *Marcus Aurelius: Meditations,* with an introduction by D. A. Rees. London: Everyman's Library.

FORSTATER, MARK. 2000. *The Spiritual Teachings of Marcus Aurelius.* London: Hodder & Stoughton, and New York: Harper Collins.

GRANT, MICHAEL. 1971. *Cicero: Selected Works.* London: Penguin.

GRIFFIN, M. T. AND E. M. ATKINS. eds. 1991. *Cicero: On Duties.* Cambridge: Cambridge University Press.

GRUBE, G. M. A. 1983. *The Meditations of Marcus Aurelius.* Indianapolis: Hackett.

HADAS, MOSES. 1958. *The Stoic Philosophy of Seneca: Essays and Letters*. New York: W. W. Norton. [Includes *On Providence, On the Shortness of Life, On Tranquillity of Mind, Consolation to Helvia, On Clemency*, and a selection from the *Moral Letters*.]

HAMMOND, MARTIN. 2006. *Marcus Aurelius: Meditations*, with an introduction by Diskin Clay. London: Penguin. [Includes excellent notes and index.]

HARD, ROBIN. 1995. *The Discourses of Epictetus*, edited, with introduction and notes by Christopher Gill. London: Everyman/Dent. [Includes the complete *Discourses*, the *Handbook*, and *Fragments*.]

———. 1997. *Marcus Aurelius: Meditations*, with introduction and notes by Christopher Gill. Ware: Wordsworth Editions.

HAYS, GREGORY. 2002. *Marcus Aurelius: Meditations*. New York: Modern Library.

HICKS, C. SCOTT AND DAVID V. HICKS. 2002. *Marcus Aurelius: The Emperor's Handbook*. New York: Scribner.

HICKS, R. D. 1931. *Diogenes Laertius: Lives of the Eminent Philosophers*. Vol. 2. Cambridge, MA: Loeb Classical Library, Harvard University Press.

HIGGINSON, THOMAS W. 1890. *The Works of Epictetus, Consisting of His Discourses, in Four Books, the Enchiridion, and Fragments*. Boston: Little, Brown, & Company.

———. 1944. *Epictetus: Discourses and Enchiridion*. Roslyn, NY: Walter J. Black.

———. 1948. *The Enchiridion: Epictetus*, with an introduction by Albert Salmon. Upper Saddle River, NJ: Prentice Hall.

INWOOD, BRAD AND L. P. GERSON. 1997. *Hellenistic Philosophy: Introductory Readings*. 2nd edition. Indianapolis: Hackett. [Readings from the main schools: Epicureanism, Stoicism and Scepticism. Includes the complete text of Arius Didymus *Epitome of Stoic Ethics*, Diogenes Laertius *Lives of the Eminent Philosophers* Book 7 (Zeno), and a selection of sources from Cicero and others.]

LONG, A. A. AND D. N. SEDLEY. 1987. *The Hellenistic Philosophers*. Vol. 1. Cambridge: Cambridge University Press. [Readings from the main schools: Epicureanism, Stoicism, Scepticism, and the Academics. Includes commentaries on the readings. This is the standard primary source text. Volume 2 contains the original Greek and Latin.]

LUTZ, CORA E. 2006. *Musonius Rufus 'The Roman Socrates'*. New York: AstroLogos. [Facsimile reprint of Yale Classical Studies 10, 3–147 (1947).]

MALHERBE, ABRAHAM J. 1989. *Moral Exhortations: A Greco-Roman Sourcebook*. Philadelphia: Westminster Press.

MATHESON, P. E. 1916. *Epictetus: The Discourses and Manual*. Oxford: Clarendon Press.

POMEROY, ARTHUR J. 1999. *Arius Didymus, Epitome of Stoic Ethics: Text and Translation*. Atlanta: Society of Biblical Literature.

SEDDON, KEITH. 2005. *Epictetus' Handbook and the Tablet of Cebes: Guides to Stoic Living*. Abingdon: Routledge. [Includes the *Handbook* and a substantial commentary.]

WHITE, NICHOLAS. 1983. *Handbook of Epictetus*. Indianapolis: Hackett. [Includes the *Enchiridion* and a very good introduction to Stoic philosophy.]

MODERN SOURCES

ALGRA, KEIMPE, et. al. eds. 1999. *The Cambridge History of Hellenistic Philosophy*. Cambridge: Cambridge University Press.

ALSTON, WILLIAM P. 1967. Emotion and Feeling. In Paul Edwards. ed. *The Encyclopedia of Philosophy*. New York: Macmillan, Vol. 2, 479–86.

ANNAS, JULIA E. 1992. *Hellenistic Philosophy of Mind*. Berkeley: University of California Press.

———. 1993. *The Morality of Happiness*. New York: Oxford University Press.

ARNOLD, E. VERNON. 1958. *Roman Stoicism*. London: Routledge & Kegan Paul. [Original edition, 1911.]

BOBZIEN, SUSANNE. 1998. *Determinism and Freedom in Stoic Philosophy*. Oxford: Clarendon Press.

BRANHAM, R. BRACHT AND MARIE-ODILE GOULET-CAZÉ. 1996. *The Cynics: The Cynic Movement in Antiquity and its Legacy*. Berkeley & Los Angeles: University of California Press.

BRAUND, SUSANNA MORTON AND CHRISTOPHER GILL. eds. 1997 *The Passions in Roman Thought and Literature*. Cambridge: Cambridge University Press.

BRENNAN, TAD. 2005. *The Stoic Life: Emotions, Duties, and Fate*. Oxford: Clarendon Press.

COOPER, JOHN M. 1999. Eudaimonism, the Appeal to Nature, and 'Moral Duty' in Stoicism. In *Reason and Emotion: Essays on Ancient Moral Psychology and Ethical Theory*. Princeton, NJ: Princeton University Press, 427–48.

DILLON, J. T. 2004. *Musonius Rufus and Education in the Good Life: A Model of Teaching and Living Virtue*. Lanham, MD: University Press of America.

DUDLEY, DONALD, R. 1998. *A History of Cynicism*. London: Bristol Classical Press. [Original edition, Methuen, 1937.]

GOULD, JOSIAH B. 1970. *The Philosophy of Chrysippus*. Albany, NY: State University of New York Press

HADOT, PIERRE. 1995. *Philosophy as a Way of Life*. Oxford: Basil Blackwell.

———. 1998. *The Inner Citadel: The Meditations of Marcus Aurelius*. Cambridge, MA: Harvard University Press.

———. 2002. *What is Ancient Philosophy?* trans. Michael Chase. Cambridge, MA: Harvard University Press.

HORNBLOWER, SIMON AND ANTONY SPAWFORTH. eds. 1996. *The Oxford Classical Dictionary*. 3rd ed. Oxford: Oxford University Press.

INWOOD, BRAD. 1985. *Ethics and Human Action in Early Stoicism*. Oxford: Clarendon Press.

———. ed. 2003. *The Cambridge Companion to the Stoics*. Cambridge: Cambridge University Press.

INWOOD, BRAD AND PIERLUIGI DONINI. 1999. Stoic Ethics. In Algra 1999, 675–738.

KLEMKE, E. D. 2000. *The Meaning of Life*. 2nd ed. New York: Oxford University Press.

LESSES, GLEN. 1989. Virtue and the Goods of Fortune in Stoic Moral Theory. Oxford Studies in Ancient Philosophy 7, 95–127.

LONG, A. A. 1986. *Hellenistic Philosophy: Stoics, Epicureans, Sceptics*. 2nd ed. Berkeley & Los Angeles: University of California Press.

———. 1996a. *Problems in Stoicism*. London: Athlone.

———. 1996b. Freedom and Determinism in the Stoic Theory of Human Action. In Long 1996a, 173–99.

———. 1999. Stoic Psychology. In Algra 1999, 560–84

———. 2002. *Epictetus: A Stoic and Socratic Guide to Life*. Oxford: Oxford University Press.

MORRIS, TOM. 2004. *The Stoic Art of Living: Inner Resilience and Outer Results.* Chicago and La Salle: Open Court.

MOTTO, ANNA LYDIA. 1973. *Seneca.* New York: Twayne.

MOTTO, ANNA LYDIA AND JOHN R. CLARK. 1993. 'Tempus Omnia Rapit': Seneca on the Rapacity of Time. In *Essays on Seneca.* Frankfurt: Peter Lang, 41–50.

NAVIA, LUIS E. 1996. *Classical Cynicism.* Westport, CT: Greenwood Press.

———. 1998. *Diogenes of Sinope.* Westport, CT: Greenwood Press.

NUSSBAUM, MARTHA C. 1994. *The Therapy of Desire: Theory and Practice in Hellenistic Ethics.* Princeton, NJ: Princeton University Press.

POWELL, J. G. F. ed. 1995. *Cicero the Philosopher: Twelve Papers.* Oxford: Clarendon Press.

REYDAMS-SCHILS, GRETCHEN. 2005. *The Roman Stoics: Self, Responsibility, and Affection.* Chicago: University of Chicago Press.

RIST, JOHN M. 1969. *Stoic Philosophy.* Cambridge: Cambridge University Press.

———. ed. 1978. *The Stoics.* Berkeley and Los Angeles: University of California Press.

ROWE, CHRISTOPHER AND MALCOLM SCHOFIELD. eds. 2000. *The Cambridge History of Greek and Roman Political Thought.* Cambridge: Cambridge University Press.

RUTHERFORD, R. B. 1989. *The Meditations of Marcus Aurelius: A Study.* Oxford: Clarendon Press.

SANDBACH, F. H. 1994. *The Stoics.* 2nd ed. Indianapolis: Hackett, and London: Bristol Classical Press.

SCHOFIELD, MALCOLM. 2003. Stoic Ethics. In Inwood 2003, 233–56.

SEDDON, KEITH. 1987. *Time: A Philosophical Treatment.* Beckenham: Croom Helm.

SELLARS, JOHN. 2003. *The Art of Living: The Stoics on the Nature and Function of Philosophy.* Aldershot: Ashgate.

———. 2006. *Stoicism.* Chesham: Acumen.

SHARPLES, R. W. 1995. Causes and Conditions in the *Topica* and *De fato*. In Powell 1995, 247–71.

———. 1996. *Stoics, Epicureans and Sceptics.* London: Routledge.

SHERMAN, NANCY. 2005. *Stoic Warriors: The Ancient Philosophy Behind the Military Mind.* New York: Oxford University Press.

SIHVOLA, JUHA AND TROELS ENGBERG-PEDERSEN. eds. 1998. *The Emotions in Hellenistic Philosophy*. Dordrecht: Kluwer.

SORABJI, RICHARD. 2000. *Emotion and Peace of Mind: From Stoic Agitation to Christian Temptation*. Oxford: Oxford University Press.

SØRENSEN, VILLY. 1984. *Seneca: The Humanist at the Court of Nero*. Chicago: Chicago University Press.

STEPHENS, WILLIAM O. 1996. Epictetus on Stoic Love. *Oxford Studies in Ancient Philosophy* 14, 193-210.

STOUGH, CHARLOTTE. 1978. Stoic Determinism and Moral Responsibility. In Rist 1978, 203-31.

STOWELL, MELANIE CELINE. 1999. *Stoic Therapy of Grief: A Prolegomenon to Seneca's 'Ad Marciam, de Consolatore'*. Ann Arbor, MI:UMI Dissertation Services. [PhD dissertation, Cornell University: UMI number 9941194]

STRIKER, GISELA. 1991. Following Nature: A Study in Stoic Ethics. in *Oxford Studies in Ancient Philosophy* 9, 1-73. Also in Stiker 1996, 221-80.

———. 1996. *Essays on Hellenistic Epistemology and Ethics*. Cambridge: Cambridge University Press.

TAYLOR, RICHARD. 1992. *Metaphysics*. 4th ed. Englewood Cliffs, NJ: Prentice Hall.

TIMOTHY, H. B. 1973. *The Tenets of Stoicism*. Amsterdam: Adolf M. Hakkert.

VERNEZZE, PETER J. 2005. *Don't Worry, Be Stoic: Ancient Wisdom for Troubled Times*. Lanham, MD: University Press of America.

WEBSITES

The author's MA Programme in Ancient Philosophy
http://www.warnborough.ie/faculties/arts/maancient.htm

The author's PhD Programme in Ancient Philosophy
http://www.warnborough.ie/faculties/arts/phdancient.htm

The author's article on 'Epictetus' in the Internet Encyclopedia of Philosophy [includes a Stoic Glossary]
http://www.utm.edu/research/iep/e/epictetu.htm

Translations of Stoic Texts

Epictetus' *Discourses* only (Long translation)
http://www.constitution.org/rom/epicdisc.htm

Epictetus' *Discourses, Handbook* and *Fragments* (Higginson translation, including original notes)
http://www.perseus.tufts.edu/cgi-bin/ptext?doc=Perseus%3Atext%3A1999.01.0237;layout=;loc=disc%200.0;query=toc

Epictetus' *Discourses, Handbook* and *Fragments* (Long translation, including original notes)
http://www.perseus.tufts.edu/cgi-bin/ptext?doc=Perseus%3Atext%3A1999.01.0236&layout=&loc=disc%200.0&query=toc

Epictetus' *Handbook* (Carter translation)
http://etext.library.adelaide.edu.au/mirror/classics.mit.edu/Epictetus/epicench.html

Epictetus' *Handbook* (Higginson translation)
http://www.geocities.com/khs10uk/enchiridion.htm

Epictetus' *Handbook* (Long translation)
http://www.ptypes.com/enchiridion.html

Epictetus' *Handbook* (Matheson translation, but only the first 38 chapters)
http://www.humanistictexts.org/epictetus.htm

The Golden Sayings of Epictetus
http://classics.mit.edu/Epictetus/goldsay.html

Marcus Aurelius' *Meditations* (Long translation)
http://classics.mit.edu/Antoninus/meditations.html

Marcus Aurelius' *Meditations* (Long translation) with chapter numbers and search facility
http://members.tripod.com/ptypes

Seneca's complete ethics corpus including the *Moral Letters*, and Cicero' *De Officiis*
http://www.stoics.com/books.html

Seneca's *Letters to Lucilius* (excerpts)
http://praxeology.net/seneca.htm

Seneca's *Moral Letters* (selections)
http://www.molloy.edu/sophia/seneca/epistles/index.htm

Seneca's *On Anger* (selections)
http://www.molloy.edu/sophia/seneca/anger.htm

Seneca's *On Benefits*
http://www.gutenberg.org/etext/3794

Seneca's *On Providence*
http://www.molloy.edu/sophia/seneca/providence.html

Seneca's *On Tranquility of Mind*
http://www.molloy.edu/sophia/seneca/tranquility.htm

Some Excellent Articles

The Ecole Initiative: Stoicism
http://www2.evansville.edu/ecoleweb/articles/stoicism.html

'Stoicism' in the Internet Encyclopedia of Philosophy
http://www.utm.edu/research/iep/s/stoicism.htm

'Stoicism' in the Stanford Encyclopedia of Philosophy
http://setis.library.usyd.edu.au/stanford/entries/stoicism/

'Epictetus on How the Stoic Sage Loves' by William O. Stephens
http://puffin.creighton.edu/phil/Stephens/OSAP%20Epictetus%20on%20Stoic%20Love.htm

'Stoic Ethics' in the Internet Encyclopedia of Philosophy
http://www.iep.utm.edu/s/StoicEth.htm

Other Helpful Sites

Paul's Stoic website
http://www.geocities.com/WestHollywood/Heights/4617/stoic.html

Sophia Project
http://www.molloy.edu/sophia/sophia_project.htm

Sophia Project *Introduction to Stoic Ethics*
http://www.molloy.edu/sophia/seneca/stoicism_txt.htm

Sophia Project *The Problem of Happiness in the Ancient World*
http://www.molloy.edu/sophia/ancient_lit/happiness/contents.htm
for the Sophia Project on-line course on Stoicism
http://www.molloy.edu/sophia/ancient_lit/happiness/stoicism1.htm

St. George William Joseph Stock's *Guide to Stoicism*
http://www.gutenberg.org/etext/7514

'Stoicism' at About.com
http://ancienthistory.about.com/library/bl/bl_intro_philosophy_stoic.htm

Stoic Links
http://www.geocities.com/stoic_links/

The Stoic Place
http://www.wku.edu/~jan.garrett/stoa/

The Stoic School of Philosophy
http://www.stoicschool.com/

Stoic Serenity

A Practical Course on Finding Inner Peace

Keith Seddon

First published by Lulu 2006

© 2006 Keith Seddon

ISBN 978-1-84753-817-8

The main text of this book is set in Book Antiqua 10/14 pt. with Arial for display, and for all supplemental texts. Typeset by the author using Microsoft Word 2002; proofs checked and reviewed in Portable Document Format created using Nitro PDF Professional 4.91.

The illustrations are from *Hope's Greek and Roman Designs*, Dover Publications 2005, excepting those on pages 8 and 188, which are from *Costumes of the Greeks and Romans*, Dover Publications, 1962.

Quoted extracts from copyrighted sources have been used in accordance with the principles of 'fair dealing' ('fair use' in the USA) providing for the legal, non-licensed citation or incorporation of copyrighted material in another author's work under which an author is not required to ask permission of copyright holders, but must ensure that titles and authors of the works quoted appear in either the text itself or in an acknowledgements page, such that (in an agreement between the Society of Authors and the Publishers Association) a single extract of up to 400 words or a series of extracts, of which none exceeds 300 words, to a total of 800 words from a prose work may be quoted from copyrighted material for purposes of criticism, scholarship or review (see the Society of Authors publication, *Quick Guide: Permissions*, at <http://www.societyofauthors.net/soa/page_id.php4?pid=104&sid=16&urlsection=Publications>). All sources are fully cited and listed in the Bibliography. Sources still in print are readily available from booksellers. Quoted sources have been carefully chosen with the intention and hope that readers of this work will be interested to acquire copies of the source books.